Curriculum Studies Worldwide

Series Editors

William F. Pinar
Department of Curriculum and Pedagogy
University of British Columbia
Vancouver, British Columbia, Canada

Janet L. Miller
Teachers College
New York, New York, USA

Aim of the series

This series supports the internationalization of curriculum studies worldwide. At this historical moment, curriculum inquiry occurs within national borders. Like the founders of the International Association for the Advancement of Curriculum Studies, we do not envision a worldwide field of curriculum studies mirroring the standardization the larger phenomenon of globalization threatens. In establishing this series, our commitment is to provide support for complicated conversation within and across national and regional borders regarding the content, context, and process of education, the organizational and intellectual center of which is the curriculum.

More information about this series at
http://www.springer.com/series/14948

Oscar Koopman

Science Education and Curriculum in South Africa

Oscar Koopman
Cape Peninsula University of Technology
Kuils River, South Africa

Curriculum Studies Worldwide
ISBN 978-3-319-82177-1   ISBN 978-3-319-40766-1   (eBook)
DOI 10.1007/978-3-319-40766-1

Cover illustration © Henk Badenhorst /Getty Images

Printed on acid-free paper

This Palgrave Macmillan imprint is published by Springer Nature
The registered company is Springer International Publishing AG
The registered company address is: Gewerbestrasse 11, 6330 Cham, Switzerland

To my late father, Andreas Willem Koopman, who always believed in me.

FOREWORD

My first engagement with the author on a personal level was as a critical reader for his doctoral dissertation. I must admit that reading his dissertation then and this book now is not an easy task, as he always draws his ideas and knowledge frameworks for his work from the complex field of philosophy, psychology and subfields such as science education. Through many other personal discussions with the author, I came to know him as a critical scholar with a deep sense of purpose, which is to humanise the teaching and learning of science. This book endeavours to do just this and is a long-overdue guide for in-service science teachers, preservice teachers and teacher educators in South Africa.

Developments in Africa (and in South Africa) depend critically on the effectiveness of its mathematics, science and technology programmes. This is because these disciplines drive the technological and scientific innovations in the rest of the world and are central to a nation's economic growth. It is for this reason that major monetary investments are made in a country's education system. Despite initiatives to support the development of science through heavy monetary investments and research by entities such as the African Union and the World Bank, Africa contributes roughly 5% to the world's gross domestic product (GDP) compared to the USA's 17.1%, and it holds 0.1% of the world's patent rights compared to 23.6% of the USA. South Africa is the second largest economy on the continent and contributes 0.7% to the world's GDP and holds less than 0.01% of the world's patent rights. These statistics are directly related to the quality of the country's mathematics and science programmes.

This raises a very important question: How effective are South Africa's mathematics and science programmes?

This book is an attempt to answer this important question and gives an indication of what is happening in the teaching and learning of science in South African classrooms. It addresses critical elements such as the nature of the physical science curriculum over the last five decades (Chap. 2), the teachers' disposition towards curriculum change (Chap. 4) and the nature of teacher content knowledge (CK) and pedagogical content knowledge (PCK) (Chap. 5) and offers some interesting suggestions on how to improve the quality of teaching and learning of science in South Africa.

Steven Biko speaks in all his work about the importance of a 'critical consciousness of blacks' in order to reclaim the self as a subjective epistemological being in the racial malaise of the South African context. Chapter 3, in a dialogue between father and daughter, captures all the essential elements in this book. First, there is his nine-year-old daughter's disposition towards the content she is taught by her Grade-4 teacher and how she (the daughter) displays a critical stance towards the information. Second, the role of the teacher in the teaching process is discussed and the way that she (the teacher) decries change with respect to her practice and knowledge in post-apartheid South Africa. Although the latest Curriculum and Assessment Policy Statement dictates that teachers should act like catalysts to awaken the creativity and curiosity of learners with the aim of instilling a critical consciousness in them, the teacher is still stuck in an authoritative and instrumental paradigm that aims to produce—to borrow a term from the author—'robots'. This dialogue also captures the essence of the author's positionality in the data-construction process and his thinking in which he skilfully puts on his phenomenological cap to elicit further details from his daughter. This approach is also the predominant methodological and data-explication framework for the book to describe the state of science teaching and learning in South Africa.

In summary, in Chap. 1, the author develops an overarching framework for applied phenomenology for science teachers. This lays the foundation for the methodological and data-explication framework for almost all of the chapters. His aim is to humanise science teaching and learning, with a strong focus on the 'object pole' as opposed to the 'ego pole' by using experience both as the starting point and as the end point in researching the activities of science teachers.

Chapter 3 narrates the author's personal life journey from childhood to being a university student of science and the impact of the values instilled in his consciousness on his later life as a teacher and teacher educator of physical science. Here he provides the reader with deep insight into the impact and significance of apartheid education as he elucidates the inner tensions he grappled with to overcome firmly held (unconscious) beliefs. This journey is central to his development of a critical consciousness, hence his critical scholarship with respect to science teaching and learning. This narrative articulates his becoming and exemplifies Steve Biko's notion of 'a critical awareness of the self'.

Through the eyes of Thobani, in Chap. 4, we get a sense of the lived experiences of many black physical science teachers in the new South Africa. It accentuates his life journey as a learner and as a science teacher and will resonate with so many physical science teachers in the country who were exposed to 'horrible science teaching' under apartheid. At the same time, the author cautions in-service teachers of the potential impact that a teacher can have on his learners and society by being what Thobani refers to as destroyers of dreams. This chapter also explains how black teachers grapple with the implementation process because of dialogical tensions that could arise with older colleagues and heads of departments who resist change and as such hinder curriculum change. The phenomenological methodological framework allowed me to understand to a certain extent what so many new graduates might be going through.

Chapter 5 addresses a critical question: *Do teachers also see what chemists see when they teach science?* This chapter unpacks the CK and PCK of 15 teachers that is essential for effective science teaching. As this book speaks to heart of the science teacher, another underlying question is: *Do learners also see what chemistry teachers see when they sit in their science lessons?* In order for this to happen, teachers of science should have strong CK as well as PCK. This will help teachers to make better didactical decisions with respect to their science teaching, all informed by a strong science content base.

In Chap. 6 the author looks to the outside world to see in what way a wine expert can contribute to the teaching of science. The author now observes and engages with a wine expert to see what lessons could be learnt for the teaching of science. These lessons are eloquently captured in his critical reflection of the wine expert's lived experiences to bring his approach to learning about the sensory properties of wine into the science classroom.

An important element of the teaching process is what is at play when decisions are made around the development of school curricula for school subjects. Chapter 2 speaks about the abuse of power. The author rightly warns that government has an obtrusive role aimed at policing the curriculum process rather than working towards empowering learners for a science for life. The concluding chapter asks the question: *Can a phenomenological approach enhance learning in science in South Africa?* This question is critical for readers and especially science educators in the South African context. Dwindling numbers for the subject in the final three years of schooling for Grades 10–12 necessitate a new look at the teaching of science. This is the contribution the book makes to the field of science education; let us be bold in exploring this approach in all spheres of science education to follow a 'science for life' approach in which teachers harness the full use of the senses to empower our learners. This book touches a critical nerve for us all to take a conscious decision to contribute in this regard to reclaim the rightful academic space of science education in South Africa.

Wellinggton, South Africa   Kalvin Whittles

PREFACE

To get some idea of the current state of science teaching in South Africa, I asked five physical science education specialists from different provinces to describe in one sentence what they think the main reason is for the poor performance of learners in the subject. Unsurprisingly, all blamed the teachers. Three of the five in agreement said, 'It is because teachers do not understand the content.' The other two said, 'Teachers do not understand the curriculum' and 'Teachers do not know how to teach the content effectively.'

These views raise serious issues, and this book brings all these concerns together—by design and by coincidence. First of all, the book explores the impact of the socio-historical, political and economic environment in South Africa on the physical science curriculum, which in turn impacts on the nature of science teaching. This is because both during and after apartheid South Africa school science took an interest in a specific kind of didactical approach and knowledge, which the book refers to as 'a science of government'. This 'science of government' approach leaves the learners with a blurred sense of the foundations of science that is disconnected from external nature and human nature and is presented as a series of abstract concepts and definitions. Six of the eight chapters investigate the dialectical tensions between the physical science curriculum and the teacher in his or her role as an active implementer of the curriculum as planned. By drawing on the work of various phenomenological scholars, such as Edmund Husserl, Martin Heidegger, Merleau-Ponty and Max van Manen, the book is an attempt to describe the lived experiences of the science teacher to unpack these tensions.

The following is the brief synopsis of the book. Chapter 1 introduces the reader to phenomenology as a potential methodology to research the lived experiences of science teachers as opposed to the dominant quantitative approach to research for the last two centuries. The author provides a succinct account of phenomenology with respect to its philosophy, data-construction methods and the data-explicitation process. Chapter 2 examines how the 'governmentality' of the apartheid and post-apartheid governments established the pedagogical and knowledge discourses that constrain the intellectual development of physical science learners in South Africa. Chapter 3 chronicles the lived experiences of the author under apartheid as a learner and university science student and then as a science teacher in post-apartheid South Africa. This chapter discusses the impact of the behaviourist core values instilled into his consciousness under apartheid at primary school, secondary school and as a university science student on his later life as a science teacher. The chapter also discusses his 'unbecoming' and how he had to unlearn deeply embedded values to repudiate most of his previously acquired formal learning *about* science. Chapter 4 recounts the lived experiences of a black physical science teacher and his struggle to implement a new curriculum. This chapter reveals how lack of support from the Department of Education and his head of department retarded the implementation process. It also highlights the difference between 'curriculum as planned' and 'curriculum as lived'. Chapter 5 investigates the content knowledge of 15 physical science teachers on selected topics in the science curriculum. The focus of this chapter is on investigating whether they include all three levels of representation in chemistry when they teach a topic: macroscopic, microscopic and submicroscopic levels. Chapter 6 explores the lived experiences of a wine expert and how he acquired his knowledge about wine. This chapter also discusses what science teachers can learn from the wine expert and offers the experience of a wine expert's approach as an analogy to learning science. Chapter 7 valorises the use of the senses in the science classroom and offers science teachers alternative teaching strategies, referred to as sense-experience approaches, to enhance the use of the senses in the science classroom to assist learners to codify, analyse and construct knowledge. The concluding chapter reports on an investigation into the question of whether a phenomenological approach can enhance the quality of learning in science. The study critically compared the rationale, approaches and outcomes of various other didactic approaches to teaching and learning in science education in South Africa.

This book carries with it an enormous debt of gratitude to many indi-viduals, some of whom cannot even be named. I must begin by expressing my gratitude and appreciation to William Pinar, also grateful to Lesley Le Grange, who introduced me to William, which I see as where the book initially started.Chapter 4 is a revised version of the article I published with Lesley Le Grange and Karen de Mink in the journal *Education as Change*. Therefore, I would like to thank the journal for giving me per-mission to do so.

There are some persons to whom the successful completion of this book was directly related and to whom I am happy to express my gratitude here. For the critical but always helpful and insightful comments and sugges-tions, I want to thank Albert Harold and Edwin Hees for their outstand-ing editorial work. To my wife, Karen, who has been my Rock of Gibraltar. Finally, to my two daughters, Taffi and Phoebe, who inspire me always to give my best.

Kuils River, South Africa   Oscar Koopman

CONTENTS

LIST OF FIGURES

LIST OF TABLES

CHAPTER 1

Phenomenology as a Method in Education Research

D'Agnese (2015), in a thought-provoking article entitled 'The inner [and unavoidable?] violence of reason: Re-reading Heidegger via education', alludes to the powerful influence of Western thought on modern-day discourses on knowledge production. He draws from Heidegger when he writes,

> Since Plato, Western thought has framed knowing as a procedure within 'some realm of what is' and a predetermined 'sphere of objects'. This method erases its own traces, presents this reduction as unavoidable, and establishes that 'human beings' 'stand-over-and-against' the world. (D'Agnese 2015, 435)

Today, this trend still persists, both nationally and internationally, in which science education researchers put too much emphasis on the mathematical nature of knowledge and consequently lose its roots in lived experience. In other words, knowledge is framed in some mathematical procedure that ignores the importance of human relationships and lived experience. Since these mathematical transformations of knowledge proved to be very successful for many centuries, researchers have become more and more obsessed with them (Dahlin et al. 2009). Consequently, this paradigm of 'knowing' dominates modern discourses, including human science research in which human behaviour is converted into mathematical formulas and lived experience loses its central epistemic position and described as mathematical models of truth. To this end, researchers reduce

© The Author(s) 2017   1
O. Koopman, *Science Education and Curriculum in South Africa*,
DOI 10.1007/978-3-319-40766-1_1

their research participants to mere objects, and their findings are seen as more real than the concrete, lived experiences from which they have been abstracted. Husserl (1970, 59) calls this the 'technisation' of scientific knowledge. He avers that this technisation involves a gradual sedimentation of meaning in which lived experience is ignored (or forgotten) in favour of mathematical conceptualisations. He writes,

> ... This problem of forgetfulness is exacerbated by the fact that with each new generation's inheritance of the new techniques—an inheritance that presupposes the processes of transformation without explicitly recognising them—another increment in the Selbstverständlichkeit [matter of course] of natural scientific achievement occurs as well (Husserl 1970, 59).

According to Dahlin et al. (2009), the 'sedimentation of meaning' relegates mathematical formulas to a higher level than lived experiences, and by doing so mathematics takes on a form of its own. When this happens, science replaces the concrete lifeworlds of individuals with abstract mathematical models and formulas that people find strange and difficult to understand. Landau (1997) explains how mathematics and science were reinforced and popularised in the seventeenth and eighteenth centuries in the West. He avers that in the course of these centuries, rationalism and the enlightenment's critical and sceptical spirit spread among comparatively large sections of the population and how Newtonian science was popularised for the uneducated. Although these long-standing traditions of discourse and practice have solidified and cannot be transformed in an instant, the development and establishment of alternative discourses are needed to gradually change things.

Dahlin et al. (2009) assert what is needed to change these dominating trends and traditions of knowledge and knowing is an ontological reversal in our approach to research. They point out that an ontological reversal occurs when experience-as-lived is elevated to a much higher level than mathematics. In other words, what is secondary ontologically becomes primary. This means a complete transformational shift from cognitive reductive abstraction to a more phenomenological description of reality and nature. If this shift takes place, the knowledge is justified by the approach adopted towards acquiring it.

This brings me to the aim of this chapter, which is to argue for a shift to a phenomenological approach to conducting research into the practices of science teachers. As a method, phenomenology brings together the theory and practice of science teaching and reverses the order of priority of the ontological (being) and epistemological (knowing) aspects of human existence as revealed in the lived experience. I will argue that phenomenology is systematic and rigorous enough to research the lived experiences of science teachers with a high degree of accuracy. Drawing on the work of Husserl and Heidegger, this chapter highlights the value of phenomenology in revealing the natural attitudes of research participants as they emerge in the phenomenological reduction deeply embedded in the consciousness of individuals. A related aim is to guide novice researchers in how to use phenomenology in the data-construction process and also how to explicate phenomenological findings without contaminating the data with extraneous presuppositions, strongly held beliefs or preconceived ideas and notions based on the researcher's own worldview. I start by explaining my journey in discovering phenomenology as a potential research method in science education.

MY JOURNEY IN DISCOVERING PHENOMENOLOGY

In a paper entitled 'Phenomenology as a potential research methodology for subjective knowing in science education research', I paint a picture of my research journey in search of an appropriate methodology to research the subjective lived experiences of science teachers in South Africa. In this article, I draw on the work of Husserl, Heidegger, Merleau-Ponty and van Manen, among others, to recount my personal engagement with how I discovered phenomenology as a research method to frame my doctoral study. I describe this search—to borrow from Pinar (2004)—'as the nightmare that is present' as I engaged with the work of these scholars and various other phenomenological scholars. Indeed, the difficulty of the text of these phenomenological scholars and my obligation to keep on looking, reading and tarrying in search of a rigorous methodology evoked feelings of confusion as well as misinterpretations and misreading. However, what motivated me to continue searching and reading this 'complex language' and 'terminology', as Cerbone (2009) puts it, was the rewarding insights the work of these scholars gave me. For example, phenomenology made explicit my own thoughts about life, human actions, behaviours of people and their intentions. It also helped me to become more thoughtful and tactful in my role as a science teacher (and later researcher) to be more 'caring' and 'sensitive' to the other. From this experience I could relate to Pinar and Reynolds' (1991, 2) claim when they describe their own encounter with phenomenology when they write that instead of 'having found something' they 'have been found'. To them, Heidegger's and Husserl's work made their sky visible in its entirety in a metaphorical sense.

Each time the meaning of the writing of different phenomenological scholars distilled and eventually settled in my mind, I realised the value of phenomenology simply not as a research methodology but as a philosophy to understanding human lived experiences. This engagement with phenomenology liberated me from the constraints of positivistic thinking. To support this claim, I wrote, "Like a bird released from a cage, I experienced science anew and recognised the viability of phenomenology as a research methodology that would assist me in answering my research question..." (Koopman 2015, 4).

I learned that what separates phenomenology from other methods is that it does not offer the possibility of a theory with which researchers can explain the world of participants, but rather it offers the possibility of bringing the researcher into closer contact with the world of the participant (Van Manen 2007). In other words, phenomenology moves away from the researcher as an outsider in search of data in favour of the researcher as an active participant in generating knowledge. This means the phenomenologist brings sensitivity to the field of educational research, something which, according to van Manen (1990), has been long overdue. I also learned when entering the data-construction field, it is not about me but about the participant and that I have an ethical responsibility to report his or her experiences in their fullness, richness and greatest depth. To do so I had to be perceptive and avoid the dangers of being misled, sidetracked or enchanted by extraneous elements and had to avoid getting carried away by unreflective preconceptions and personal emotions. So instead of theorising about my participants, I had to bring out the significance of their voices as they describe their lived experiences as science teachers in contemporary South Africa. This brings me to the question: what is lived experience?

Epistemological Foundations of Lived Experience

Merleau-Ponty (1962) describes *lived experience* as an embodied act that manifests in time and space. This embodied act is centred on the thesis that an object is perceived in relation to the horizon within which it is embedded and from which it stands out. Horizon refers to those pure acts that are impressed on human consciousness. In other words, experience is the body's connectedness to concrete physical things that surround it. Husserl (1980, 2), in agreement with Merleau-Ponty, goes a little further and describes experience as a lived-through event that is immediate and prereflectively fixed in the consciousness of the person. For example, when we observe a tree, the tree as it is observed is a concrete physical object that is presented to the person as a self-given unperceived awareness that has no awareness of itself. This awareness as revealed by the object in experience, according to Van Manen (1990, 36), can never be "grasped in its immediate manifestation but only reflectively as past presence". In the first instance 'past experience' does not mean experiences from the past that are gone but instead refers to those experiences that were experienced in the past whose presence presents themselves to the mind in the present. This means that instead of conceiving the object the moment it is observed, its true meaning is revealed through a process of reflection. Husserl (1980) describes these temporal horizons as the unity of events obtained in our consciousness as a unified experience of both past and present. This means the spatial and temporal aspects of lived experience are disentangled by defusing the historical and the incidental structure of experience. When this happens, the fullness and richness of the essences of the experience are revealed from which inferences or deductions are drawn. For this reason, the focus in lived experience is on the textual expression of the essence of the experience to grasp the true (intended) meaning of lived experience.

Experiential Event Versus Experience

Peirce via Strand (2014, 436) asserts that experience is "the total cognitive result of living". In agreement with Husserl, he believes that all knowledge has its origin in experience. The act or embodiment of experience as presented to human consciousness and the perceived aspects as perceived in the event are what separate experience from the experiential event. To corroborate this statement, Pierce (1905) writes, "Experience and an experiential event are … utterly different, experience being the effect that life has produced upon habits" (in Strand 2014, 436). To Pierce (1905), a sensation is not the same thing as an experience because experience is a consequence of the effect that life has produced upon habits. I will now draw on an example to explain the difference between an experience and an experiential event. The experiential (event) of tasting wine for the first time is different from the effects that the taste produces (experience event) and the consequential act of tasting on our habit. The experience can be described as the person lifting the glass filled with wine with his or her hands to bring the wine into contact with his or her tongue to taste. This experience is followed by a reflective process to generate sensations. In what follows sensation can be described as a conscious reflection that produces habit (Strand 2014). From this experience the wine taster constructs his or her own perceptions about the taste of wine that is intuitively given. This 'intuitively given' articulation of experience, according to Husserl (1980), precedes all knowledge and thinking.

The Significance of Lived Experience in Science Education

Researching *lived experience* is to express the essence of experience. This is not about gathering facts and information about people's lives but more about learning what can be learned from the lived experience of others which presses upon their minds every moment of every day (van Manen 1990). By 'learning' here I mean to 'report' and 'explicate' the structural nexus and motif that gives experience its specific meaning with a high degree of accuracy, depth and richness. The structural nexus is the patterns or units of meaning that form the unifying whole in a particular contextual setting through a process of reflection. This approach to research is a philosophy *in* experience and falls within the ambit of phenomenology which aims to describe the lived world of the research participant. As a philosophy, phenomenology is not interested in how children learn science, but rather what is the essence or nature of the experience of learning science from their point of view (Van Manen 1990). The nature or essence of the learning experience provides deeper insight into the effect of a particular learning experience on a child as opposed to how they learn. Lived experience does not need any interpretation because, according to Husserl (1970, 1980), the interpretation already exists *in experience.*

In science education most researchers ignore lived experience and approach their research from a quantitative methodological standpoint. This is because the researcher views the nature of teaching and learning as a wholly conceptual problem. This approach under discussion here immediately shifts the focus of the problem to an experiential challenge and not to experience. For this purpose, the analyses of the findings are incomplete as they exclude or ignore the voices of the researched. This consequently narrows the research problem down to particular instances or what phenomenologists call 'severing the whole' and the analysis reports the effects of 'units of the experience' on teaching and learning. In other words, quantitative researchers report the fragments instead of the unified whole to show the significance of the conditions around the teaching and learning process. From this perspective, Pinar and Reynolds (1991, 2) describe quantitative research as an *'evil character'* that aims to quantifying the immeasurable. To do this, as a researcher in their view is unethical and epistemologically unsound:

> The firmament in the positivist sky twinkles with precision and rigour. However, the spaces between stars and those hidden by clouds recede and disappear. Phenomenology seeks to name those spaces, their relation to the stars and to us. The unity in the epistemological whole resides in ourselves (Pinar and Reynolds 1991, 2).

According to Heidegger (1977), in phenomenology the answer to understanding what is (the phenomenon) lies at the foundation of our existence. To get to the phenomena does not require the application of some method or methodology, but in being and what it means to be. Heidegger's being stands in strong contrast to empirical or positivist science and other human sciences, where the search for understanding rests on a reduction of truth found in the sphere of objects. In other words, according to Heidegger *'dasein'* (meaning *being there* or *there being)*—a notion which I will unpack later in this chapter)—has nothing to do with a method or a plan but rests on lived experience.

Husserlian Phenomenology

Phenomenology as a method is effectively summed up by Husserl's famous dictum that it is essential to return to the things themselves *(zu den Sachenselbst)* (Husserl 1975, xix). Husserl explains this dictum when he writes, "We must not make assertions about that which we do not see ourselves" (*Ibid*, xix). *Sachen* in German does not refer to physical objects but rather to subconsciously held ideas. These subconsciously held ideas have their roots in those personal experiences that matter most to us. According to Husserl (1975, xix), the only way to access these subconsciously held ideas or structures of knowledge is through a consciousness unburdened with preconceived ideas or notions derived from the individual's personal experiences or perceptions. This approach, according to Husserl (1975, xxii), generates "pure presentations or uninterrupted sense data" derived from experience. Husserl firmly believes that an individual's consciousness is reflected in his presence in the world, which represents his or her intentionality—that is, the directness of his or her consciousness towards the object of thought. What is required from a phenomenologist in the field is to behave like someone who is watching and enjoying a film, without analysing its aesthetic, sociological and technical aspects. When the film is finished, the analyses must be carried out objectively and independently of any emotional involvement and unsubstantiated criticism. Husserl uses the phrase '*epoche*' to explain the process of bracketing the self. In his view, this bracketing refers to the mathematical principle of bracketing an equation. By implication, that which is inside the brackets has no connection with any terms and numbers outside of it. In other words, the experience as divulged in a conversation must be treated as an indubitable 'givenness' that represents an individual's consciousness free from opinion or correction. In research, this means that during the data analysis, the researcher enters a totally presuppositionless space by suspending all possible interpretations and meaning. This requires the researcher to read each respondent's transcriptions with openness and to enter the individual's world in order to extract meaning from what the person is saying. It must be stated that at times this is difficult because each participant has his or her own unique way of experiencing temporality, spatiality and materiality, but each of these co-ordinates must be understood both in relation to others and to their own inner world (Hycner 1985, 29).

Given the complex structures and notions of Husserl's thought, phenomenology could be a minefield to novices. The reason is that although phenomenology does not make use of inductive techniques, it is not entirely independent of them. However, in the data-collection process (which I explain in more detail later in the sections to follow), any experience must serve as foundation data in order for the researcher to arrive at a clear understanding of the lived world of individuals. In other words, according to Husserl (1977), mental acts, including the objects in the person's memory, point towards some *Sachen* or matters of importance that are external to the individual. These matters of importance are presented to individuals as an object-for-a-subject. These experiences become intermeshed with an ever-present pure consciousness leading to the observer constantly having to re-examine existing perceptions. Therefore, reality or the lived world of individuals can rightly be said to be external to the observer, just as the reader of a book is external to the book itself (Husserl 1975, xxi).

HEIDEGGERIAN PHENOMENOLOGY

Heidegger's (1967) magnum opus *Being and Time*, dedicated to Husserl, developed his ideas further and adopted an ontological stance towards his philosophy of phenomenology. His focus tended more towards the nature of being rather than 'becoming to know'. Here Heidegger rekindles the debate about the meaning of what he terms *dasein*. Heidegger believed that consciousness is not separate from the world but that it is a formation of historically lived experiences. Heidegger believed that people are self-interpreting beings—that to live is to listen and to derive meaning from experience. Heidegger (2002) attempted to understand and explain the nature of shared meaning among human beings and what a culture gives a person from birth as a way of understanding the world. He strongly believed in the importance of context, which he defined as time and space. His notion of phenomenology is inductive and descriptive by nature and focuses on, or recognises, the importance of the subjectivity of experience.

Science education research, that involves human beings, is construed as a necessary and imperative move away from positivistic and interpretive paradigms that speak directly to the object pole. It is through the ego pole (the element of consciousness) that human beings can see and grasp the essence of a phenomenon. The transition from the object pole to the ego pole brings us closer to an understanding of what is really happening in the mind of the individual or what Husserl (1977) considers to be the truth. Heidegger (2002, 8) avers that truth speaks of 'unhiddenness'. He argues that unhiddenness refers to that which is no longer hidden or has been torn away from hiddenness (*Verborgenheit*). In his view, truth has little to do with factual context but rather reveals the unhiddenness that speaks about directedness arising from fundamental experiences in the real world (ibid, 5–7).

THE VALUE OF PHENOMENOLOGY AS A RESEARCH METHOD

As alluded in the previous sections, for Husserl (1983, 5) cognition begins and ends with experience. Gadamer (1975, 34) argues that experience has a condensing and intensifying meaning. He maintains that the totality of experience is found in the significant whole. This significant whole refers not only to a person's presence but to his or her complete presence. Husserl (1975, xiv) notes that this whole or unity of an object is something that is given among various appearances and not something separate and alongside them. It is considered a structural nexus that is contextually connected to reflect upon so as to give it a significant quality of meaning. Therefore, according to Husserl, phenomenology is a form of inquiry that describes the lived experiences of others and informs us about the participant's perceptions of not only a physical object. These perceptions provide phenomenological researchers with the necessary intellectual tools to understand human behaviour and actions and to do something about the latter when necessary.

In view of the above, phenomenology is both a theory and a method. Its epistemological and ontological disposition is predicated on the lived world or lived experiences of individuals. As a methodology, its ontological representation suggests serious and original thinking about how individuals perceive or understand the world. The essence of a phenomenological study is the endeavour to answer the question of what it means to be (Groenewald 2004; Heidegger 1967). Answering this question requires an active science with a unique methodology. In such a paradigm, the attitude of the researcher should not be superior to that of the participant's understanding of the world. According to Heidegger (1967, 38), the essence of being (*dasein*) lies in existence. The question of existence can only be addressed through 'existing', which means that it is the only way through which our existence in general can be interrogated. Heidegger invites us to think of a particular self-interpretation that a given *dasein* lives out: the existential possibility it chooses to enact as an existential understanding, which he describes as an ontic state. In other words, in Heidegger's conceptualisation of being, *dasein* provides the richest, most complete and the most revelatory way of engaging with a phenomenon in fundamental ontology. In this way, people gain an understanding of what it is that they comprehend about a particular phenomenon.

Dasein, or the search for understanding about understanding, can be considered a non-methodological journey whereby the researcher enters a space (domain) of personalness that calls for a personal engagement with the participants (Heidegger 1967, 41). This is critical because the participants' description of the world must be rendered in their own words, as distinct from the researcher's own verbal account of it. Instead, the subjects themselves must verbally construct their personal world and the meaning derived from it in order for the researcher to understand how they experience the world. One way of ensuring this is to return each written summary of the participant's description to him or her for a validity check and to involve the participant in judging the accuracy of the researcher's description of the experience. In so doing, the participant can confirm whether or not the information has been correctly captured and whether or not corrections are needed. Furthermore, the participant should be given the freedom to add or remove information. Based on this premise, phenomenology is essentially interested in the subject's episte-mological and ontological disposition. In other words, the phenomenolo-gist asks what the truth is about this or that and strives to expresses it in an uncontaminated (unbiased) way in order to provide a rational under-standing of what it means to be using *pure data*, which is also expressed as *lived-through data*, as discussed later in this article.

Dasein is both a question of the present and the past. Our existence in its entirety includes our preceding existence; therefore, we are not only present *now* but also represent the fusion of past, present and future. It is true that past occurrences can significantly affect the present and the future. Heidegger (1967, 3) argues that the present, past and the future are the collective theme of all human phenomena of experience. A person's existence or experience cannot be accurately understood or explained without considering the present, the past and the future. For this reason, phenomenology as a method goes against the grain of the orthodox scientific attitude, which focuses on the object pole rather than on embracing the subjective world of the individual (Levering 2006, 454). For example, fear can neither be understood nor be measured. Spanos (1976) argues that the only way to understand a phenomenon (in this case, fear) would be to live in the body of the person and actually experi-ence it. Otherwise, all that we can observe is an inner self that shows up on the outside but can never be understood. This is not to say that interpre-tive, quantitative and mixed methodologies cannot produce trustworthy or reliable data, but these methodologies are inadequate for the purposes of describing or converting the data into fixed writing accurately. Any real-life event cannot be perfectly captured in writing because language has limits as it cannot describe moods and emotions accurately. This accords with Derrida's (1967) thesis that there is no stability in language and that it therefore cannot accurately describe an event or experience because dis-positions such as mood and phenomena such as fear and sadness cannot be captured in language (4). The person who aims to describe or report a phenomenon is forced to reduce the content in some way so that oth-ers might understand the phenomenon. 'Embodiment', as described by Merleau-Ponty (1962), may be of some help here. In Merleau-Ponty's world, a person normally projects meaning that is constituted only in that person's own world. Meaning for Merleau-Ponty (1962, 112) is 'summoning', which refers to a sense in which the medium summons and causes an absent person to appear.

For the most part, in the present things such as the disposition of mood and context are absent, leading to a misrepresentation of truth. In Heidegger's (2002, 45) view, evidence becomes doubtful and can be regarded as everyday opinions if we take our histories as something forgotten. For Heidegger, it is only when the individual's background (context/ontology) or historicity is foregrounded that the visible becomes meaningful and truthful. Therefore, a consideration of both the past and the present allows the voice of the participant to be reliably reported or represented. The inner voice of the participant becomes the first-person data needed to arrive at a proper understanding of the person's real, lived-in world. So, with specific reference to the research context of science education, instead of trying to theorise about the activities/behaviour of teachers 'objectively', it is about studying teachers and not so much about teaching science. To do so, the researcher should allow the subjective nature of phenomenology to reflect the uniqueness and essences of the lifeworld of science teachers with deep sensitivity. This raises the question of how the uniqueness of a participant can be rendered in a trustworthy manner and how phenomenology embraces this uniqueness.

DATA-CONSTRUCTION METHODS

In the scholarly tradition, interviews and field notes are considered the best ways of collecting phenomenological data. Through interviews the essential nature of a phenomenon is sought. Allowing the participants to divulge their lived experiences gives them an opportunity to reflect on their own practices (Geneallos 1999; Taylor 2001; Sadala and Adorno 2003; Groenewald 2004; Tan et al. 2009).To maintain the rigour of a phenomenological investigation, there are features of the purposes and styles of interviews that distinguish them from other research approaches.

The Phenomenological Interview

According to Nijhof (1997), researchers use interviews as a looking glass to capture the lived-world experiences of their research participants. Lemke et al. (2006) view phenomenological interviews not as being as simple and straightforward as a 'looking glass' but rather as indicating a blurry and messy, dynamic flow of events that social science tries to corral into a deceptive neatness in the place of reality as a primary experience. This is because reality is messy and contingent to 'some' meaning when all is said and done. Lemke et al. (2006) draw on Halliday's three major orientations of interviews: ideational-thematic, interpersonal-attitudinal and organisational-logical. Ideational-thematic, he explains, presents us with the world as a state of affairs. The ideational-thematic focuses on role of the person in the world as he or she is enmeshed in everyday processes, actions and relationships to others under unique circumstances in time and space. This forms the foundation for the interpersonal-attitudinal function which construes our action in terms of speakers and addressees, rhetorical functions and speech acts, degrees of intimacy and formality, superiorities or deference, attitudes to others (such as participants) and our attitude towards the ideational-thematic content of what we are talking about and our relations to those we are talking to. The organisational-logical dimension brings the ideational-thematic and the interpersonal-attitudinal together as wholes or parts as they emerge from the interview and is translated to text. This interview text focuses on the organisational units its strands of cohesion running across the boundaries of those units. This interview text, according to Lemke et al. (2006, 84), enables us to define the nature of the relationships, those key aspects we talk-into-being, additive and concessive, superordinate and subordinate, extensions and elaborations, and so forth. Each of these aspects is key to understanding how science teachers and learners make meaning about their lives. Therefore, an interview is not just talk or conversation but a search for meaning and understanding about the lived world of research participants. The phenomenologist is fully aware that reality is multi-scaled in time and space as it is projected across our experiences—not just in different moments but a unity of those moments. Therefore, the interview not only searches for the macro-reality as divulged in the conversation but the micro-reality that reveals the phenomenological attitude of a research participant. For this reason, Dinkins (2005) alludes to the way in which the researcher enters the thoughts and feelings of their participants, because this influences the rigour and depth of the data-construction process.

Interviews can take place one-on-one or in groups, depending on the aim and the underpinning philosophy of the research design. Today different types of research interviews are conducted in qualitative research, including focus group, unstructured or semi-structured interviews. Each

Table 1.1   Research philosophy and open-ended interviews

Philosophy	Influence
1. Ontology:	To what extent does the researcher believe that an objective reality exists beyond that constructed by individuals involved? Concerns about interviews are directed by premises about whether what is being collected corresponds with reality or is in some sense a construction of reality.
2. Epistemology:	To what extent does a researcher believe that reality can be constructed through a data-gathering process such as interviewing? For example, are interview data representative of respondent's beliefs and values or are they a construct of what the respondent believes the researcher should hear?
3. Inquiry:	What is the role of the researcher? To gather data dispassionately or to engage with the respondent in constructing an account of the phenomena (ethic or epic inquiry)?
4. Deduction or induction:	Is the role of research to test or create theories? Inductive interviews that are open in style may be used to map the phenomenon, while deductive interviews partially structured may be used to assess the significance or volume of phenomena.
5. Data-gathering analysis:	Interviews may be guided by an incremental analysis of data from previous interviews or conducted with no prior review of past transcript data. Interview data may be seen as an outcome (result) or resource.

Source: Sadala and Adorno, 2003

interview type has its own objective and its unique underpinning philosophy. Price (2003, 1) summarises how the research philosophy directs and guides a particular choice of interview. Table 1.1 presents the research philosophy of open-ended interviews and how each interview type is influenced by its specific philosophical considerations.

Table 1.1 represents the different underpinning philosophies that guide an interview. It not only explains how different interviews guide and direct researchers but also explains how the questions must be framed or structured. The different philosophies guiding the interview in Table 1.1 also reveal that interviews do not produce data about research participants but about the whole interview that are just as much data about the interviewer and the relationships they co-constitute with the research participants. In the phenomenological interview, the interviewer introduces topics unanticipated and engages in genuine dialogue and not in some superficial pseudo-conversation that belongs to repertory forms of dialogue.

In Husserl (1970) phenomenology, the focus is on epistemology, where the interviewer seeks to uncover deeply embedded subconsciously held ideas and beliefs as divulged in the conversation. This is because Husserl had an epistemological view of the world, which he inherited from Cartesian dualism in which he views the mind as separate from the body. Husserl moved away Cartesian dualism as he was more interested in discovering the truth about the world and humans which he believed can be accessed through understanding lived experience. Husserl (1970) avers that lived experience can be explored systematically through rigorous inquiry by allowing the research participant to recount his experience of a specific event. To remain true the phenomenological paradigm—and to shift away from positivist thinking—the researcher must remain open to unexpected or unfamiliar responses to make room for interactive exchange to manifest. To do so, two important principles must be adhered to in interview process: *epoché* and *essence*. To explain *epoché* Husserl (1967, xix) writes, "We must not make assertions about that which we cannot see." *Epoché* is the Greek word for bracketing, and therefore, the phenomenologist focuses on any part or all of the experience by removing the self from the experience. This means the researcher must focus only on data divulged in the interview. Essence (*wesen* in German) refers to the way the research participant experiences a phenomenon. In other words, the researcher must construct the interview questions to exhaust the phenomenon under investigation. Both these terms guide the behaviour of the researcher in the data-construction field. By applying the principle of the *epoché*—that is bracketing the self from all preconceived ideas and interpretations by allowing the participant to communicate freely—the dialogue on the *essence* of the study is kept fluid and dynamic to uncover and generate meaning rather than reconstrue understanding. Bracketing the self and focusing on the essence reveal the *eidos* or *eidetic residuums* of the research participant, which refers to the subconsciously held ideas and beliefs about the phenomenon under investigation.

Heideggerian (1967) phenomenology, on the other hand, focuses on the ontological aspects of a person's existence in the world and his or her representation of reality. The focus is on the epistemic nature of human consciousness, whereas the Husserlian tradition provides insight and comprehension of the human condition as lived. Here the focus is on the lifeworld without resorting to any categorisation or conceptualisation and often includes questions that elicit responses and information that are often taken for granted by other research paradigms. On the contrary, in the Heideggerian tradition, the focus is on *dasein* (Heidegger 1967). *Dasein* is translated as the mode of being human or the situated meaning of a human being in the world. In the Heideggerian tradition, the focus is on the 'self' in order to exclude many assumptions and prejudices as a possibility to explain the type of human being we have become (Cerbone 2009). So in the Heideggerian (1967) interview the researcher must approach the interview with the aim of drawing out the preontological conceptions that the research participant hold about the world. This means the focus is not on understanding the research participant's consciousness but rather on everydayness that is constantly projected through *dasein*. So what kinds of principles or guidelines guide the researcher?

In the Heideggerian interview, the focus is on describing the world of the research participant through interpretation. In other words, as the research participant's story unfolds, the interpretation process begins. An important goal of this interview is to make sense of the individual's experiences. This is because Heidegger (1967) believed that people cannot refrain from preconceived notions about the world, and therefore, the researcher becomes an agent involved in the interpretative process. This means the researcher can describe the mood and atmosphere around the interviewees. Other aspects include the impact of history, religious and dominant cultural identities, and how different role players shape or influence the participant's thinking. By doing so, the researcher emphasises that *dasein* is already projecting and manifesting in experience. This is because to Heidegger nobody is free from *dasein*, and it is the researcher's responsibility to orientate the interview in such a way that will reveal implicitly held values and beliefs that will answer the main research question.

Interview Techniques

Artful interviewing takes place when the researcher knows and understands the ways in which people's actions, thoughts and beliefs correspond with each other. As such, the *laddered technique* of interviewing is advised by Price (2003, 3). This technique selects the most appropriate level of questioning and researcher response to the dialogue. Laddered questioning operates on three levels, namely (1) inviting questions, that is, questioning that is aimed at setting the scene for the interview in which the researcher makes the respondent feel comfortable and relaxed. This creates the impression (in the research participant) that the researcher is interested in and cares about what they have to say; (2) knowledgeable or invasive questions are asked later in the interview when the respondents have shown signs of relaxation or comfort. This involves questions such as What do you think? How do you feel? By showing empathy, sensitivity and interest in the participant's responses, trust is established between the researcher and respondent; and (3) questions of personal philosophy. These are the most invasive questions as they focus on beliefs, values and deep-seated feelings. This also forms the core of the interview and allows the researcher insight into the respondent's personal identity. Asking questions at this level is akin to asking questions about *who you are* and may leave the respondent feeling that the researcher is judging them. At this point, the researcher's body language must be positive because any negative movements, facial expressions or statements made by the interviewer can affect the responses obtained. To display positive body language Finlay (2009) suggests that the researcher must not become preoccupied with participants' experiences of an encounter. By preoccupied I mean not being in any way judgemental, hence distancing the self from the participants' stories of their lives.

In addition, the researcher must pay careful attention to the participant's embodied selfhood and how he or she relives those moments through his or her stories in relation to other actors in the story. For example, if the respondents are teachers, how do they articulate their relationship with their peers, learners and parents? This reveals how they execute their duties as teachers and the relational responses to their learners in the science classroom. This is where the researcher's expert knowledge in the field guides his or her understanding of the research participant's world. To remain true to the phenomenological circle of data construction, another approach would be for the researcher to place himself or herself in the shoes of the teacher in an attempt to view the world of the teacher through his or her own experiences without any form of bias. According to Seidman (2006), the key to conducting any interview is through effective listening skills, which I will discuss next.

Listening Techniques

According to Seidman (2006), listening attentively is a skill that all human science researchers must cultivate before conducting (phenomenological) interviews. According to van Manen (1990), interview data are more effective when the researcher remains silent between questions as the conversation proceeds forward. Out of this space of silence, he notes, the researcher offers a more reflective space to the participant. Silence avoids the researcher filling the conversation with unnecessary awkward chatter that might distract the participant. The silence also makes the researcher be more finely attuned to the participant's responses and focus solely on what is being said, to discern what may be hidden in the conversation and to adopt a sensitive position to the cadence of the interview. By remaining silent and listening attentively to the participant's story, the researcher can capture the facial expressions, small hesitations or micro-body movements (often in the eyes, hands and feet) more clearly. So instead of steering the conversations away from what is being said, attentive listening assists in helping to decode the information accurately. Effective listening requires an open and positive attitude that motivates the participant to divulge more detail and depth about an experience.

Field Notes

According to Miles and Huberman (1984), taking field notes (or memoing) as a method is an important source of data construction for phenomenologists. Field notes are considered as a secondary data-construction process. These are the sense data that the researcher records while in the field constructing his or her data. Field notes zoom in on what the researcher hears, sees, feels and thinks in the course of the data-construction process. They give insight into the deeper emotional expression of the participant and capture the mood and atmosphere in which the interview is conducted.

Emerson, Fretz and Shaw (1995, 1) assert that the researcher must be alert and observant of non-verbal cues (namely the length of the pauses between responses, facial expressions, attitude and behaviour) displayed by all research participants during the interview process. Field notes reflect the knowledge of what goes on in the mind of the participant. Therefore, it is important to make notes during the interviews to keep the field notes fresh. Groenewald (2004) cautions researchers that, when they record field notes, the best time to write notes *is no later than the morning after.*

This is where the phenomenologist must be cautioned in the way he or she reflects on and presents the field notes. According to Husserl, it is important to bracket out the researcher's views and values from the way the data are constructed or interpreted. The voice of the participant in the data-construction process is central in a phenomenological framework. Phenomenology focuses on the consciousness of the mind or experiences as given by the research participant, and hence, the researcher must bracket out anything outside or inside himself or herself to explain the essence of each participant's intentional objective.

EXPLICATION FRAMEWORK OF INTERVIEW DATA

Husserl's work on phenomenology was entirely focused on the theoretical and philosophical aspects of lived experience. He left no recognisable step-by-step approach or formula to practically explicate the data. This is because the aim of Husserlian phenomenology is to report the raw and unprocessed data in the form of statements concerning the underlying intersubjective intuitions or consciousness of the respondents by using mostly the direct words of the research participant. Van Manen (1990, 53) notes that "the notion of data is ambiguous within the human science perspective" and adds that when the data are explained, the explanation must be "objectively constructed". To remain true to the Husserlian tradition is to abstain from any form of interpretation and to present the data as a descriptive narrative as divulged in the interview.

Heidegger's (1967, 2002) philosophy allows the researcher to present an interpretive narrative of the lived world of each research participant. The interpretive narrative gives meaning to the interview data by peeling away layer by layer the external voices of each research participant that represents the natural attitude to reveal the phenomenological attitude of the participant. This starts with the researcher sterilely reading the transcriptions to get the feel of the whole interview. This involves meticulously scrutinising each word, phrase, sentence and paragraph in the interview transcripts in order to distil the true nature and essence of each participant's everyday involvement with the world. The interview as a whole provided a context for the emergence of specific meanings and events. From this, the researcher deduces the fundamental reasons why the individual research participants behaved the way they did or said what they said. This unveils the tangible structures of their experiences. By combining the researcher's expertise and knowledge in the field with the reality of the research participants as depicted in the transcription, he can unveil how personal events unfolded in the lives of the participants. Next, I explain step by step how to analyse a research participant's interview transcript.

The Transcript Analysis

Giorgi's (1985) method involves the following four steps:

1. The researcher must first get a sense of the whole interview to get a holistic picture of the lived world of the participant. To do so, the researcher must read the transcript over and over until he or she

captures or grasps the main ideas that point to the crux of the interview.

2. The next step is to construct *natural meaning units* (NMUs) about the phenomenon under investigation. This requires the researcher to bracket the self and not to misrepresent the main ideas of the participants.

3. The NMUs should be interpreted for their essential meaning, which is restated by the researcher in psychological text, to present the ontological clues and ideas. At this point, the NMUs are converted to transformed meaning units (TMUs) that allow the researcher to create a narrative of the participant's life.

4. The structuring the narrative involves the synthesis of the TMUs into a consistent statement of the structure of teaching or learning, and so forth, by drawing from theories and theorists for corroboration and substantiation. Here the researcher's synthesis integrates the ideas and insights contained in the transformed meaning into a consistent description of the psychological structure of the event.

Constructing the narrative

1. The researcher establishes priority themes, derived from the text by using the formula **frequency** × *int*ensity, to construct the narratives. In this formula, *frequency* refers to the repetition (continuous) use of words and phrases that dominate the text, whereas *intensity* refers to strong descriptive words in order to identify the invariant structure of experience. These words provide the basis for the narratives.

2. The narrative is divided into two parts. The first part uses Husserlian phenomenology, also called descriptive phenomenology, where mostly the direct words of the participants are used in which each participant's story is narrated. This can be in the form of a succinct biography or summary of the participant's life. The descriptive narrative, according to Much (2006, 51), explores and reports how the story unfolds from its opening to its closing statement. It is important to summarise the whole story so that the reader can get a full sense of the participants' response.

3. The second part draws on Heideggerian phenomenology, or interpretive phenomenology, in which key aspects in descriptive phenomenology are now highlighted and divided into a more specific theme that highlights both what goes on inside the mind and what goes on the classroom of each participant. At this point, the researcher can draw from his personal experience as an expert in the

field or literature on psychological theories as the main argument that will answer the research question.

As phenomenologists it is impossible to think that we can access with absoluteness what is inside the 'heads' of teachers and learners because every interpretive narrative is really a description about a larger system. For example, in the case of the teachers, it is the conditions in which they work, such as the infrastructure of the school, availability of resources, the curriculum, support from local district offices, the learners, the role of parents, and so forth. In the case of the learners, it is the socio-economic conditions in which they are raised, culture of the school, quality of teaching and learning, personal beliefs and values, and so forth. None of these factors is static and permanently present as they represent a fluid and dynamic landscape in which the individual functions. In other words, the interpretive narrative is always presented as some contingent description with reference to what a research participant can do and not what he or she 'knows' in some 'complex, interactive situations with all resources at hand, other people, artefacts and their own bodies' (Lemke et al. 2006, 89). Thus conceived, what phenomenology offers is a synoptic meaning of the lived world of the participant with no predictive value.

CONCLUSION

This chapter has explained phenomenology in all its complexity as a research method. By drawing from my journey in discovering phenomenology as a research method, I have shown why it is important that novice researchers in the field of phenomenology must first become well acquainted with the theoretical framework and its complex methodology before applying it. This chapter also indicates how novices might enter into the lifeworld of teachers and remain open and attuned to the complexity and unpredictability of their inner lives. From this standpoint, I stresses the importance of returning to lived experience to lay bare human consciousness in order to represent the lives of teachers or learners as accurately as possible. It points out how phenomenology embraces the common features of the essence of human experience and views experience and behaviour as being locked in an integral and inseparable relationship (Moustakas 1994, 8). In this regard, phenomenology focuses on the structure and the variations of the structure of consciousness (Giorgio 1989). It provides a theoretical description of lived experience as revealed primarily through the consciousness of an individual, without any intention to justify, explain or interpret the experience.

Husserl (1975, 1977) has shown that, as a research methodology, phenomenology is rigorous and intellectually precise in that it allows the data to flow freely from the research participant to discover the immediate consciousness from which the structure of experience and the fundamental epistemological facts about a phenomenon derive. By bracketing out the researcher's dogmatic beliefs, judgements and preconceived ideas, the self purifies the unadulterated apprehension of experience and allows the researcher to see the participant as a unique individual. Husserl's phenomenology has great potential for science education, and his methodology articulates a scrupulous commitment to the research participant's voice insofar as it represents a passionate commitment and insight in order to educe the meaning that expresses our essential existence as human beings. I also explain why this is so and builds a case for the application of phenomenology in science education.

Finally, I explained the role of the researcher in the data-construction process with specific reference to the phenomenological interview, the phenomenological relation between the researcher and the research participant during the interview and the different steps involved in the data-explication process. Phenomenology, unlike in natural science, elevates lived experience above mathematics and transports the researcher beyond what he or she can see as it becomes a way of seeing that has the potential to change our thoughts about the world. The shift towards phenomenology creates an ever-opening space of knowledge rather than presumptuous interpretations of the lived world of our research participants.

REFERENCES

Cerbone, D. (2009). *Understanding phenomenology*. United Kingdom: Acumen Publishing Limited.

D'agnese, V. (2015). The inner (and unavoidable?) violence of reason: Re-reading Heidegger via education. *Journal of Philosophy of Education, 49*(3), 435–455.

Deleuze, G., & Guattari, F. (1987). *A thousand plateaus: Capitalism and schizophrenia*. Minneapolis: University of Minnosota Press.

Derrida, J. (1967). *Writing and difference*. London: Routledge.

Dahlin, B., Østergaard, E., & Hugo, A. (2009). An argument for reversing the bases of science education—A phenomenological alternative to cognitionism. *Nordina, 5*(2), 201–2015.

Dinkins, C. (2005). Shared inquiry: Socratic-hermeneutic interpret-viewing. In P. M. Ironside (Ed.), *Beyond method: Philosophical conversations in healthcare research and scholarship* (pp. 111–147). Winsconsin: University of Winscons in Press.

Emerson, R. M., Fretz, R. I., & Shaw, L. (1995). *Writing ethnographic field notes*. London: United Kingdom.

Finlay, L. (2009). Ambiguous encounters: A relational approach to phenomenological research. *Indo-pacific Journal of Phenomenology, 9*(1), 1–15.

Gadamer, H. G. (1975). *Truth and method.* New York: Seabury.

Geneallos, R. (1999). A review of the socio-political context of adolescent mental
health and adolescent mental health nursing in Australia. *The Australian and
New Zealand Journal of Mental Health Nursing, 8*(4), 134–142.

Giorgi, A. (1985). *Phenomenology and psychological research.* Pittsburgh: Duquesne
University Press.

Giorgio, A. (1989). An example of harmony between descriptive reports and
behaviour. *Journal Of Phenomenological Psychology, 20,* 60–88.

Groenewald, T. (2004). A phenomenological research design illustrated.
International Journal of Qualitative Methodology, 3(1), 1–27.

Heidegger, M. (1967). *Being and time.* New York: Harper and Row.

Heidegger, M. (1977). *The question concerning technology and other essays.*
New York: Harper and Row.

Heidegger, M. (2002). *Heidegger: The essence of truth* (T. Sadler, Trans.). London:
British Library of the Congress (Original work published 1988).

Husserl, E. (1967). The Paris lectures, 2nd edition. (P. Koestenbaum, Transl.).
The Hague: Martinus Njihoff.

Husserl, E. (1970). *The crisis of the European sciences and transcendental phenomenology: An introduction to phenomenological philosophy* (D. Carr, Trans.).
Evanston, IL: North-Western University Press.

Husserl, E. (1975). *The Paris Lectures.* (P. Koestenbaum, Trans.). The Hague:
Martinus Njihoff.

Husserl, E. (1977). *Phenomenological psychology* (J. Scanlon, Trans.). The Hague:
Martinus Njihoff (Original work published 1962).

Husserl, E. (1980). Phenomenology and the foundations of the sciences (T. Klein
& W. Pohl.). The Haugue: Martinus Njihoff Publishers.

Husserl, E. (1983). *Ideas pertaining a pure phenomenology and to a phenomenological philosophy* (F. Kersten). The Hague: Martinus Njihoff (original work published in 1913).

Hycner, R. (1985). Some guidelines for the phenomenological analysis of interview data. *Human Studies, 8,* 279–303.

Koopman, O. (2013). Teachers' experiences at implementing a new science curriculum. Unpublished doctoral dissertation. Stellenbosch University.
Stellenbosch.

Koopman, O. (2015). Phenomenology as a potential methodology for subjective
knowing in science education. *Indo-Pacific Journal of Phenomenology, 15*(1),
1–13.

Landau, I. (1997). Why has the question of the meaning of life arisen in the last
two and a half centuries? *Philosophy today, 41*(2), 263–269.

Lemke, J., Kelly, G., & Roth, M. (2006). Forum: Towards a phenomenology of
interviews. *Cultural Studies of Science Education, 1,* 83–106.

Levering, B. (2006). Epistemological issues in phenomenological research: How authoritative are people's accounts of their own perceptions? *Journal of Philosophy of Education, 40*(4), 451–463.

Merleau-Ponty, M. (1962). Phenomenology of perception (C. Smith, Trans.). London: Routledge and Kegan Paul.

Moustakas, C. (1994). *Phenomenological research methods.* Thousand Oaks, CA: Sage.

Much, C. (2006). The art and craft of rigorous analysis and authentic (re)presentation. (report). *Qualitative Research Journal, 6*(1), 51–64.

Miles, M. B., & Huberman, A. M. (1984). *Qualitative data analysis, a sourcebook of new methods.* Newbury Park, CA: Sage.

Nijhof, G. (1997). Response work: Approaching answers to open interviews as reading methods of research for social scientists. *Qualitative inquiry, 3*(2), 169–188.

Pierce, C. S. (1905). The basis of pragmatism in phaneroscopy. In N. Houser (ed). The essential Pierce, vol 2. Selected philosophical writings (1893–1913). Bloomington: Indiana University Press

Pinar, W. (2004). *What is curriculum theory?* Mahwah, NJ: Erlbaum.

Pinar, W., & Reynolds, W. (1991). Curriculum as text. In W. Pinar & W. Reynolds (Eds.), *Understanding curriculum as phenomenological and deconstructed text.* Kingston New York: Educator's International Press.

Price, B. (2003). Laddered questions and qualitative data research interviews. *Journal of Advanced Nursing, 37*(3), 273–281.

Sadala, M. L. A., & Adorno, R. d C. F. (2003). Phenomenology as a method to investigate the experience lived: A perspective from Husserl and Merleau-Ponty's thought. *Journal of Advanced Nursing, 37*(3), 282–293.

Seidman, I. (2006). *Interviewing as qualitative research: A guide for researchers in sensitive pedagogy.* London Ontario: University of Western Ontario.

Spanos, V. W. (1976). Heidegger, Kierkegaard and the hermeneutic circle: Towards a postmodern theory of interpretation as dis-closure. *Boundary, 4*(2), 455–488.

Strand, T. (2014). Experience is our great and only teacher: A Peircean reading of Wim Wenders' wings of desire. *Journal of Philosophy of Education, 48*(3), 433–444.

Tan, H., Wilson, A., & Olver, I. (2009). Ricoeur's theory of interpretation: An instrument for data interpretation in hermeneutic phenomenology. *International Journal of Qualitative Methods, 8*(4), 1–15.

Taylor, C. (2001). Patients' experiences of feeling on their own following a diagnoses of colorectal cancer: A phenomenological approach. *International Journal of Nursing Studies, 38*(6), 651–661.

Van Manen, M. (1990). *Researching lived experience: Human science for an action sensitive pedagogy.* London: Althouse Press.

Van Manen, M. (2007). Phenomenology of practice. *Phenomenology & Practice, 1,* 11–30.

CHAPTER 2

Physical Science: A Science for Government or a Science for Life?

INTRODUCTION

The aim of this chapter is twofold: that is, to distinguish clearly between the constructs 'science for life' and 'science for government' as applied to the teaching of physical science and to demonstrate that physical science as an academic subject offered as an elective in the Further Education and Training (FET) band in South Africa is designed to serve as a 'science of government' and not as a 'science for life'.

'A science for life' approach refers to 'knowledge *in* science' that stimulates creativity and critical thinking. Learners are encouraged to ask questions about why objects behave in a specific way, make predictions and carry out investigations to refute or validate the predictions. In other words, the focus is not only on scientific knowledge per se but on how knowledge in the scientific world is developed, with a focus on the scientific method and real-life applications. Thus, the classroom experience cuts across all three domains of learning, namely 'the self and being', 'knowledge and knowing' and 'acting and practice' (Gredley 2015, 257). A 'science for government' approach, by contrast, treats knowledge *about* science as being mainly cognitive, conceptual and static. Consequently, the subject matter is presented in an abstract manner that is foreign to the lived world of the learners. This does not mean that the knowledge offered in physical science is false and unreliable or that the learner will not benefit from it, but rather that it creates a way or framework of thinking that limits the learner's understanding of the world. Central to this conclusion

© The Author(s) 2017
O. Koopman, *Science Education and Curriculum in South Africa*,
DOI 10.1007/978-3-319-40766-1_2

is the belief that the learners are not trained at school level to operate as prospective future scientists.

To elucidate this contradistinction, this chapter first explains how the practices of successive governments during the apartheid and post-apartheid eras resulted in unsymmetrical power relations that continue to determine the knowledge discourses and constrain the intellectual development of physical science learners in South Africa. Unsymmetrical power relations refer to the unevenness of power between government and its people (e.g. teachers and learners). This unevenness of power results in government gaining dominance over its citizens. Subsequently, government has the power or authority to decide 'what' knowledge should be taught and 'how' it should be conveyed to learners in schools. One of the main challenges facing South Africa is its position in the local as well as the global 'knowledge economy'. This is evident from the premium placed on subjects such as mathematics and physical science. The chapter draws on Foucault's concept of 'governmentality', which is explained in detail later, to examine the development of physical science in South Africa and to show how the government-designed curricula allowed their authors to gain dominance or control over the learner's thinking, resulting in the dialectical negation of the learner in the process. Consequently, neither the learner's needs nor his or her understanding of the physical world is given any consideration in the teaching and learning process. Secondly, the chapter compares the different physical science curricula in force during the apartheid regime and subsequent democratic dispensation in terms of their similarities and differences to demonstrate that the focus has not been on empowering the learner with scientific knowledge, which continues to stunt the intellectual growth of the learner. As a point of departure, the chapter examines the nature of power as an access point to understanding the discourses and practices that learners are subjected to.

FOUCAULT AND THE NOTION OF 'POWER'

Power, according to Foucault (2002), symbolises a relationship between partners that have a specific nature. He writes, "… A relationship of power is a mode of action that does not act directly on others, rather, it acts upon actions: an action upon an action" (Foucault 2002, 340). This means, in a society, power operates through established knowledge discourses in social bodies, organisations or institutions. As a result, individuals who are part of these social bodies or organisations are forced to obey the rules and demands stipulated as policies. In these structures, power never ceases as individuals' behaviour, attitudes or performance are assessed by the policies. Those who follow and apply these policies in their organisations are often rewarded; for example, in institutions such as schools, teachers might be promoted to a better position where they earn more money; learners progress from one grade to the next while individuals in societies are valued and commended for good behaviour. Hence, power must be analysed as something that circulates in the form of a chain. This basically means that in order to understand power we need to (1) be cognizant of the knowledge discourse that operates in societies as legitimate practices, (2) be attentive to the purpose of the discourse and (3) expose the nature of its brutality.

In tracking the different forms of rule in Western civilisations, Foucault explains how these governments were established as a form of rule or domination (*Herrschaft*) over individuals (Christie 2006). Governments, she argues, through the exercise of power, strategically legitimise specific practices to promote a particular philosophy that develops a specific 'morality' that regulates the conduct of their citizens. This Foucault (1982) calls 'the conduct of conducts', which hinges on the intensification of the objectives that governments have for their citizens. This can be explained in terms of governments' 'economic' or social agenda for their citizens. From this perspective, the object of power is government and the target of power is the citizens. Governments focus on the people in relation to their specific habits of mind, ways of acting and thinking (Foucault 1991, 93).

With regard to school science, firstly, the curriculum can be described as the 'knowledge of the state' or 'a science of government'. The practices of teachers are guided by the curriculum. This interaction between the curriculum and the teachers as the implementers, thereof, can be described as government's apparatuses and knowledge in all its different elements, dimensions and factors of power. Although the school does not represent an extreme form of government power, it serves as a basis for the operation of power and thus as a means of surveillance. In other words, it is a technique through which both learners and teachers are observed in the operation of knowledge. Continuous testing, examinations and the creation of learner profiles are all technologies of power used in this surveillance. Resistance to these control mechanisms can lead to serious challenges for both teachers and learners, such as teachers losing their jobs and learners being labelled as incompetent. Foucault (1982) uses the terms 'bio-power' and 'bio-politics' to denote this form of governmental power or governmentalities that use the teacher and the curriculum to regulate the learner's thinking and perception of the world. In this respect, the learner becomes an object though which "habit 'inhabits' the body as a form of capillary power that permeates the body and inserts itself in action, attitude, discourses' and everyday lives" (Foucault 1982, 127). In other words, a transformation of the self takes place, a process during which knowledge masks the technology of control, which is institutionalised through practices and rationalities that ultimately become as a way of life.

GOVERNMENTALITY AND PHYSICAL SCIENCE

Foucault's essay entitled 'Governmentality' presents a genealogy of the question of government and explains how governments establish successful control over their citizens (1991, 91). In this essay, Foucault alludes to the task of government in its role to establish continuity in both an upward and a downward direction. Foucault (1991, 91) writes, "This downward line, which transmits to individual behavior and the running of the state, is just at this time beginning to be called *police* ..." Governmentality dates back to medieval times (Foucault 1980). During this period, Western societies delegated all power to the ruler, whose duty it was to decide what was legal for societies to do. When the Roman Empire was reconstructed in the twelfth century, the emperor had a constitutive role to play as he had absolute power to determine the laws and rules of the empire. In European societies, not under Roman rule, the King was the "central personage in the entire legal edifice of the West" (94). In modern societies, absolute rule or domination over society has devolved from one absolute ruler to groups such as governments—that is, absolute power has been decentralised and become shared power. Foucault states that governments are focused on

> ...a sort of complex composed of men and things...men in their relations, their links, their imbrications with those things that are wealth, resources, means of subsistence, the territory with its specific qualities, climate, irrigation, fertility, and so on; men in their relation to those other things that are customs, habits, ways of acting and thinking, and so on; and finally men in their relations to those still other things that might be accidents and misfortunes such as famine, epidemics, death and so on ... (cited in Hodgson 2010, 112).

Christie (2006) explains that modern-day governments are not much different and have a similar focus for their populations. These governments, she points out, have put in place particular practices, rationalities and doctrines through which they govern, leading their populations to particular forms of 'governmentalities'. The term *'government'* (or *'governmentality'*) in a broad sense, Christie (2006) notes, refers to specific techniques and procedures that direct and shape human behaviour. They are imposed on people by governments through their practices and through a complex set of knowledge domains.

Odora-Hoppers and Richards (2011) remind us that, on the African continent, the first generation of colonialism involved conquering the physical spaces and bodies of Africans. By contrast, the second generation of colonialism involved colonising the African mind through disciplines such as education, science, economics and law. Over the past century, both nationally and internationally, science education researchers such as Jegede (1999) and Ogunniyi (1988, 1996) have shown through various empirical studies that the African child in his or her fated relationship with school science was (and still is) caught up in a complex web of power. This is because Western models of academic structure became entrenched in South Africa during the apartheid era and were uncritically embraced and promoted. Zipin et al.'s (2015) thought-provoking paper entitled 'Can Social Realism Do Social Justice?' explains how the 'knowledge of the powerful' gained the upper hand over other forms of knowledge in South African school curricula. They write, "Winners in power struggles promote their ways of knowing relative to others."

Currently, according to Pink (1990), colonialism takes up other forms, such as the testing regime through which governments continue to police and control the mindset of learners. These national and international benchmark tests for physical science discourage rather than encourage teacher's independence. These tests, which are set by governments, to a large extent, force teachers to adhere to governments' predesigned accounts of knowledge and prescribe how the content should be sequenced and paced in the classroom interphase. The 'standardisation' of tests and examinations limits teachers to the core curriculum and topics that they should deliver to their learners. Indirectly, the testing regime restricts the teachers' freedom to stimulate critical thinking among learners (Pink 1990). This absence of critical thinking, Baron (1994) argues, results in the inability of learners to become 'active, open-minded' individuals, where the emphasis is on rigorous testing of phenomena. Thomson (2002) points out that learners can be taught to think critically in one of two ways. They can study a topic directly with the assistance of a textbook or they may encounter modes of critical thinking in the course of studying material of different content. Because of a lack of time due to internal policy structures from government to produce good results, teachers are forced to rush through the content to prepare learners adequately for tests and examinations. Consequently, not enough time is spent in the classroom on promoting critical thinking through innovative teaching strategies.

On a global scale, increased pressure through capitalism imposes international benchmark assessment standards (ASs) of knowledge in science education. The implication is that the learner's knowledge and performance in science are predetermined, which is regularly monitored by and measured in terms of the internationally agreed framework of the Organisation for Economic Co-operation and Development's Programme for International Student Assessment. The annual report, Trends in Mathematics and Mathematical Sciences (TIMMS), serves the same purpose, and countries' science programmes are aligned with the demands of TIMMS because they are ranked according to the learners' performance in these tests. Ball (1993) believes that both the teacher and the learner are implicated in the power relations of the testing regime. Firstly, the teacher's autonomy becomes the learner's constraint, and secondly, the pressure of good results becomes the teacher's constraint.

The above discussion has much in common with the English philosopher Jeremy Bentham's design of a circular institutional building which he called the Panopticon. Given the cost of social services at the time, it was thought that the basic design could be used for a variety of government buildings since arranging all the available space around a central observation room would make it possible for one or a handful of officials to observe a large number of patients or inmates. Eventually, it was decided that the Panopticon design would be suitable for prisons where all the prisoners could be observed without their knowing whether or not they were being observed, thus forcing them to moderate and control their own conduct. From this perspective, Foucault refers to the operation of techniques observed and measured in these institutions as a form of knowledge of the self by the self. It is by submitting to the rules of these institutions that the individual is said to be making progress. This ideological construal of knowledge as determined by the state had its origin in nineteenth-century Britain and spread to the rest of the world (Hodgson 2010, 111). In much the same way, the Western conception of knowledge in science spread to

South Africa, which influenced the development of physical science, as will be discussed next, followed by a discussion of at the subject policies legislated both under apartheid and post-apartheid education and its impact on the learner.

HOW PHYSICAL SCIENCE AS A 'SCIENCE OF GOVERNMENT' DEVELOPED IN SOUTH AFRICA?

According to Walters (1964), physical science was introduced into South African schools in the Cape Province in the late-nineteenth century as two separate disciplines, namely chemistry and physics. These subjects, Walters (1964) points out, were born out of a combination of various factors, namely historical, economic and social factors. Of all of these factors, the historical carried the most weight due to the strong European presence on the African continent. The main idea behind its inception in schools was for Europe to build economic capacity in South Africa as in the rest of Africa. Ogunniyi (1986) explains that the main challenges facing the subject during this era in South Africa were the following: (1) the absence of a formal curriculum, (2) Eurocentric worldviews dominated the content, (3) Afrocentric worldviews were completely ignored and (4) resources such as laboratory equipment and academic materials such as textbooks had to be imported from Germany and England, respectively, prior to the 1930s (Le Grange 2008).

The narrow focus was to create a servile education system which prepared learners for the labour market. This labour-driven system, as Christie (2006) terms it, served as a basis for the 'conduct of conducts' for the development of a science of government that shaped the consciousness of the learners. This consciousness, instilled in learners through the legitimising knowledge discourse of science, prevailed for many decades until the wake-up call and establishment of a formal physical science curriculum in South Africa when the Russians launched Sputnik in 1957. Sputnik I not only revolutionised the South African physical science curriculum but also the American civilisation as a whole and the rest of the world's science programmes (Walters 1964). Stalner (cited in Walters 1964, 15–16) writes,

> On the 4 October 1957, the Russians put an earth satellite, Sputnik I, into orbit. This dramatic event was immediately noted around the world. The feeble and uninspiring beep-beep emitted by that 184 pound ball caught the ear of more people than the blast of the Hydrogen bomb. No one was

more astonished than the American public to have a positive demonstration that scientists working in the lab are ahead of us not only in most advanced theories but in the practical application to a working model.

Sputnik I became the catalyst for accelerating the development of the subject in South Africa and the USA. Sputnik I was taken as evidence that countries around the world were not doing enough to develop the scientific capacity of their citizenry. Developments abroad, Walters (1964) echoes, encouraged the South African government to improve the quality and delivery of the physical science curriculum, especially for the more gifted learners in the country.

Prior to the Sputnik I event in 1957, all the different disciplines of science had been delineated in the physical science curriculum. This delineation of the subject resulted in a shift in the knowledge aim of the subject. Firstly, all the different science disciplines (namely astronomy, geology, physics, chemistry and meteorology) became part of the physical science curriculum. Secondly, physical science became an eclectic course, and the major focus was on its value as more financial provisions were made for learners that were gifted in mathematics and physical science. Thirdly, this led to the establishment of the Transvaal Science Teachers' Association in 1962, where Dr S.M. Naudé (a scientist) stressed the importance of physical science (Walters 1964) for economic development. It was a matter of concern to him that in South Africa, more than one million Rand was spent on special education for children with disabilities, but no money at all on special education for above-average children. As a scientist, Naudé considered this to be an indirect but nevertheless extremely effective form of national suicide (Walters 1964, 18). Finally, Naudé's outcry resulted in the establishment of various science bodies in order to (1) give more attention to learners gifted in science, (2) promote collegiality among teachers to strengthen the quality and depth of the subject, (3) lay a more solid foundation for learners with mathematics and physical science (chemistry and physics) and (4) encourage institutions of higher learning to make their voices heard about the improper treatment and loss of gifted science learners.

Arguably, the state of physical science was seen as a national crisis, which sparked the development of science advisory boards for the then Minister of Education, who was responsible for establishing quality in physical science. Moreover, this further developed into the three-stream system of the Transvaal Education Department and the junior secondary syllabus of the Cape Province. Other attempts were made to address the strong reductionist overlay of the content in the curriculum, which focused only on concepts and principles that were far removed from the everyday experiences of the learners. What was absent from the curriculum—and equally important from a pedagogical perspective—was an understanding of the moral issues and their impact on the environment and its social relations.

While all these new changes and developments by government were becoming institutionalised for the white minority, the real contradiction was that black learners were experiencing Bantu Education. Bantu Education, legislated in 1953, continued to constrain the intellectual capacity of black learners and consequently prepared the black learner for the labour work force of a capitalist state (Christie and Collins 1982). This development will be discussed in the next section.

GOVERNMENTALITY UNDER THE BANNER OF 'BANTU EDUCATION'

The year 1948 marked the introduction of the racist ideology of apartheid. Apartheid laws and policies were legislated in South Africa's Constitution and in the Bill of Rights. For example, the Population Registration Act of 1950 and the Population Repeal Act of 1991 stated that every South African should be classified into one of four designated racial groups. These laws served to institutionalise inequality; discrimination on the basis of race, sex, ethnicity, disability, culture and language; and the dominance of white people over people of 'other' races. The Bantu Education Act 47 of 1953 was a segregation law that legislated racially separated educational facilities. According to Naidoo and Lewin (1998, 732), these racist ideologies led to the South African education system being divided into separate schools within the country and within the so-called self-governing territories of Venda, Ciskei, Transkei and Bophuthatswana, which were later reincorporated into the new post-1994 democratic South Africa. Within the boundaries of the Republic of South Africa, the education system was administered through the following four main departments: the House of Assembly (DET-A) for those classified as white; the House of Delegates (DET-D) for Indians; the House of Representatives (DET-R) for coloureds and a separate department for Africans (blacks), the Department of Education and Training (DET). In addition, some provinces were further divided into their own educational systems. Government invested heavily in schools and tertiary institutions for the minority white population, while the enrolment or participation of African learners in physical science at school was kept at a minimum. The African racial group was the most impoverished (Naidoo and Lewin 1998, 730; Ogunniyi 1986, 112). In 1990, only 44 % of physical science teachers were qualified to teach science (Naidoo and Lewin 1998, 733).

In 1959, government threatened to withdraw all state funding for black schools and universities. In other words, government would no longer support black schools and universities. Through Bantu Education, the government set the ground rules for education and its associated policies and had the power to train teachers as they saw fit. This led to the introduction of so-called Christian National Education (CNE) and Fundamental Pedagogics (FP), legitimised under apartheid education. Enslin (1984) points out that CNE was promulgated as a policy for white Afrikaner learners, with the aim of educating blacks for unequal participation in economic and social life. Articles 14 and 15 of the CNE policy specifically state that black education is the responsibility of white South Africa or, more specifically, of "the Boer nation as the senior trustee of the native" (Enslin 1984, 401). The aim of the racist CNE policy was the establishment of a separate and inferior education system for black people to ensure their unequal participation in economic and social life in South Africa (Enslin 1984).

According to Booyse et al. (2011), the so-called native was denied an academic education since there would be no one to perform the manual labour in the country. Mumford (cited in Kallaway 2011, 15) writes,

> The white man desired native education in order to train human tools for his economic and administrative machine and to make more efficient servants of the natives, whereas the natives desired the same education in order that they might attain an equality with and even challenge the white man in his own sphere.

The ideology of the Afrikaner[1] was to create a separate inferior education system for black people with a poor understanding of mathematics and science. In consequence, according to the Reconstruction and Development Report of 1994, under apartheid education, blacks suffered severe deficits in the area of mathematics and physical science. Firstly, the concentrated or abstract content of physical science was reduced and had very little impact on the existence and lifeworld of the black learner. This is because physical science in township schools was taught in a way that promoted only the 'fundamentals' of the content while the broader detail and applications of the content were ignored. Le Grange (2008) states that the fundamentals had a strong theoretical focus and formed the essential framework with which the teacher approached the learning environment in his or her design of classroom activities. In the process, the teacher was viewed as the one that unlocked reality for the child in the form of statements without critical discussions or analytical deliberations. Such approaches compartmentalised the knowledge of science and promoted a behaviourist philosophy. In such a system, the child was perceived to be an empty vessel waiting to be filled, that is, the passive recipient of knowledge because of the strong emphasis on content.

Indeed, Kahn (1993, 8) contends that the teaching was teacher-centred, strict, inflexible and dominated by rote learning. Furthermore, the science syllabus was outdated, sterile and overloaded with inconsequential facts that learners had to cite and recite from textbooks. At a conference held in Johannesburg in September 1993, the African National Congress (ANC) expressed concern that the physical science curriculum was very abstract and was largely unrelated to the everyday experiences of learners. Moreover, it demonstrated an excessive preoccupation with facts and memorising skills. The end result, according to the Foundation of Research and Development (1993) report, was that 47 % of whites chose physical science as a school subject when compared to 14 % of blacks. Moreover, the pass rate for whites was as high as 90 % on average and for blacks lower than 10 %.

This influenced the university entrance of black students, with about ten times more whites completing degrees in science even though they represented less than 10 % of the population (Naidoo and Lewin 1998). During the apartheid era, several criticisms were levelled against the existing structures, which discriminated against the majority of the learner population studying physical science. It was evident that Western thought dominated the approach to the subject at the time. Many of these factors arose from historical neglect and flagrant discrimination. Major innovations and interventions were required to replace the apartheid structures and the negative images and myths related to the subject. As teacher-centred pedagogies focused on transmission learning, many learners hated physical science and perceived it to be a very difficult and oppressive subject (Ogunniyi 1986; Naidoo and Lewin 1998). This happened because they had no voice in the classroom as a result of the intense focus on theory and the rigours of the extensive syllabus. Furthermore, time constraints limited the teachers' chances of doing practical work, as their main concern was to complete the syllabus to prepare learners adequately for the final examinations. The physical science curriculum during this period can be described as a 'disciplinary technology' that steered and dictated the learner to fit into a particular racial group. In other words, the curriculum was designed to make a black child feel inferior when it came to the learning of science. But what does all this have to do with governmentality?

In terms of governmentality, what stands out under 'Bantu Education' is the issue of 'governance' which shifts from the governance of a 'territory', as Simons (2007) terms it, to the governance of the 'individual'. In this form of governance, the individual is known through forms of knowledge such as biology, mathematics and physical science. Simon (2007, 111) writes, "This is a shift from power over life and death, to a focus on life, and on governing as regulation of the population." According to this citation, the apartheid government's deliberate agenda through Bantu Education can be seen as a form of 'bio-politics'—a specific form of governmental power through which governments control and regulate their individual members. This control and regulation includes issues such as their 'health, sanitation, birth right, longevity and race' (Foucault 1991, 73). In other words, through Bantu Education, black learners in the physical science classroom were socialised in a particular way through networks of power and accompanying 'rationalities'. The learner's struggle to understand Western notions of science was seen as incompetence, stupidity, idiocy, and so forth, which ultimately led them to believe that physical science was a difficult subject or that that the subject was not meant for black people but for someone else somewhere else. The apartheid regime viewed the black learner as intellectually incompetent, incapable of contributing anything significant to the knowledge economy, and therefore having no place in the extraordinarily complex world we live in. What we learn from this is when the knowledge discourse does not liberate the learner, prevailing traditions of governmentality serve as an aspect of technology that polices the subject. Just as the prisoner in the allegory of Plato's Cave can only see the shadow images cast on the cave wall, so the black learner is confronted with shadows of science, advocated as legitimated knowledge by government.

The constitutional ground rules and bill of rights determined the discourse of knowledge which in turn shaped the practices of teachers. It is important to note that through these policies government created and established a regime of practices 'underpinned by brutality of bodies and passions' (Christie 2006, 375). The position and direction these policies took is directly related to government's 'bio-political' agenda. Not being able or not wishing to be included in such forms of governance effects an exclusion despite the inclusive ambitions of policy.

In summary, under Bantu Education, physical science can be described as a science of government and not as a science for life. The next section will discuss physical science under the banner of post-apartheid South Africa. Does the subject continue to function as a 'science of government' or did the newly formed government of national unity shift the status of the subject to that associated with 'a science for life'?

PHYSICAL SCIENCE IN POST-1994 SOUTH AFRICA

In 1990, when the ANC was unbanned, the National Education Policy Investigation body used the format of policy discourses to explore different possibilities of what an education system might look like that could undo the injustices of existing policies. They argued that the new education system should be based on the values and principles that reflected the broader democratic movement in the country. This policy format was maintained in the Implementation Plans for Education and Training, co-ordinated by the ANC's Education Desk and the Centre for Education Policy Development (Christie 2006). Numerous academics and individuals from various academic institutions endorsed the values of the mass democratic movements. Civil society groups and non-governmental organisations made recommendations for new policy discourses and frameworks that would bring about change. These policy recommendations were lobbied for by the various stakeholders but were not considered by the New Government of National Unity because the 'People's Education' agenda of the 1980s, as Chisholm and Fuller (1996) point out, "did not constitute a coherent set of policies" that could be considered for future policy priorities. The reason is that education for the masses posed serious challenges because it was flawed in its conceptualisation of policy and policy processes. These policy recommendations also misjudged the situation at grassroots level (de Clercq 1997). Although these early policy formulations were well-intentioned, they were ignored in the end. According to Le Grange (2015), the newly formed government decided to address the inequalities of the past by

1. introducing a so-called new national curriculum framework and
2. discriminating in its funding to schools so as to benefit poor schools.

This gave birth to the Department of Education's Curriculum 2005 (C2005) (DoE 1997) and all the Department of Basic Education's (DoBE) other curricula that followed in its wake, for example, the Revised National Curriculum Statement 2005 (RNCS) (DoE 2002), the National Curriculum Statement (NCS) (DoE 2006) and government's latest Curriculum and Assessment Policy Statement (CAPS) (DoBE, 2010), all of which were regarded as the educational route out of the sterility of apartheid education. The first problem is that these national curriculum frameworks had the same underlying approach to curriculum planning as the apartheid curriculum. These so-called different curriculum frameworks were a combination of lighter or heavier touches of the 'factory' model of schooling inspired by Frank Taylor (1911). According to Le Grange (2015), Taylor's emphasis was on designing industrial systems that aimed at achieving the aim of manufacturing specified products. This was reproduced in the objectives-driven curriculum models and was evident in the government's new outcomes-based curriculum and all other post-apartheid curricula. The emphasis in this design of curriculum was on assessment. Central to such instrumentalist approaches to all these curricula was the belief that the learner and his or her lived world should be placed at the centre of the teaching and learning process (DoBE 1997; 2003; 2006; 2008; 2010), hence mandating that *subjectivity* become the ideological cornerstone of education in South Africa. How this mechanistic and instrumentalist approach was reflected at the classroom interface is another issue and of less immediate relevance and importance than the question in what way these new developments affected the teaching and learning of science.

The main problem facing the teaching and learning of science was that the post-apartheid government had failed to break with past practices and rationalities. For example, although there were major changes in terminology, from aims and objectives to outcomes and assessment protocols, the principles of the curriculum framework remained unchanged. This is illustrative of what Le Grange (2015) calls "change without a difference". He argues that the differences between the apartheid and post-apartheid curricula were only semantic, which he aptly terms "transformation rhetoric". Honan's (2004) study had found that science teachers only engage rhizomatically with policy—that is, some adopt policy, some resist it, while others subvert it. Consequently, any change that took place at the classroom interface can be described as symbolic rather than 'real' (see, Basson and Kriek 2013; Jansen 2002; and Koopman 2013).

In 2009, another attempt to address the inequalities of the past resulted in the National Norms and Standards for School Funding to be amended (Le Grange 2015). Hence, schools were divided into five national quintiles (NQs) based on three poverty indicators: income, unemployment rates and the level of education of the community in which the school is located. NQ 1 represents the poorest schools and NQ 5 the wealthiest schools. Today, schools situated in affluent areas with an NQ 5 rating charge exorbitant school fees. These so-called high fees schools provide smaller class sizes because the schools have enough funding to employ additional governing body posts. In a visit to a private school earlier this year, the researcher observed that the teacher pupil ratio was as low as 1:17 for learners enrolled for physical science in Grade 10 and 1:12 for Grades 11 and 12. These observations by the researcher are also congruent with the findings of a study conducted in affluent schools in Stellenbosch by Le Grange et al. (2012). Another advantage these schools have is that they can afford the services of well-qualified and experienced physical science teachers. They are also well-resourced and subjects such as physical science remain popular among learners. Compared with these NQ 5 schools, the NQ 1 schools situated in peri-urban townships and deep rural areas have teacher pupil ratios ranges of between 1:40 (Koopman 2013). Research conducted in these schools shows that the schools in these neighbourhoods are poorly resourced and learners get very little exposure to practical work (Basson and Kriek 2013; Koopman 2013; Le Grange 2015). Furthermore, teachers are poorly trained and find the teaching of the content challenging. According to Basson and Kriek's (2013) survey, 88 % of the teachers they sampled in township schools had not received any formal training in teaching physical science for Grades 10–12. It follows that the learners that are most negatively affected are the African learners situated in peri-urban informal settlements and rural areas.

Furthermore, researchers object to the latest version of the national curriculum, the CAPS, on the grounds that it is too prescriptive and retrogressive—'retrogressive' because, as in the past, it gives teachers little space for innovation and critical discussion of the content. It prescribes what is to be taught and when and how it should be taught. The 2014 and 2015 physical science National Senior Certificate (NSC) results have shown that the introduction of CAPS resulted in no significant improvement in the performance of learners and that despite numerous humbling, high-cost efforts by government, the status quo remains. In addition, various influential sources such as the Umalusi Report of 2014 noted with concern the rapid decline in the number of learners enrolled for physical science from 2012 to 2014 as compared with previous years.

CONCLUSION

This chapter explored the question whether physical science as an academic subject in South African schools is designed to serve as a science of government or a science for life. The findings show that the design of the physical science curriculum during the apartheid era as well as after the transition to democracy did not aim to prepare young learners to become scientists. In order to promote a science-for-life approach, the learner should be introduced to the fundamentals about how scientists work and should be introduced to the scientific community to know what will be expected of them as future scientists. Drawing on Foucault's construct of 'governmentality', it is argued that both teachers and learners are exposed to physical science as 'a science of government' that merely promotes knowledge about science. The treatment of physical science as a science of government, coupled with the effect of policing and control through the learning and testing regimes, stifles the intellectual development of learners and the innovative and creative abilities of teachers. This form of social control renders the learner incapable of arriving at a full understanding of the self and his or her relationship to the world. Using Foucault's concept of governmentality, the chapter has also argued that in South African schools the aim of teaching science is not to liberate the learner for his or her own personal growth but to maintain social relations of power. Throughout this chapter, the link between governmentality, power, control, surveillance and physical science has been demonstrated by providing insight into government's objectives for the learner. This 'technology of learning' functions to police rather than to empower the learner. As illustrated in this chapter, this evidence-based regime determines what knowledge is permissible and impermissible. This dominant discourse prevalent in South African schools replaces the human qualities of intellectual integrity, insight, wisdom, common sense, passion and experience with a static content-based rote-learning approach to learning science. Just as in the allegory of Plato's Cave, the prisoners could only see the shadows, we see the 'illusions' of science without understanding the knowledge of science. In other words, our knowledge of science resembles distortions that are strung together like a pattern of appearances that we are made to believe is reality.

REFERENCES

Ball, S. J. (1993). Education policy, power relations and teachers' work. *British Journal of Educational Studies, 30*(12), 106–121.

Baron, J. (1994). *Thinking and deciding* (2 ed.). Cambridge: Cambridge University Press.

Basson, I., & Kriek, J. (2013). Are grades 10–12 Physical Science teachers equipped to teach physics? *Perspectives in Education, 30*(3), 110–122.

Booyse, J. J., Le Roux, C. S., Seroto, J., & Wolhuter, C. C. (2011). *A history of schooling in South Africa: Method and context.* Pretoria: Van Schaik.

Chisholm, L., & Fuller, B. (1996). Remember peoples education? Shifting alliances, state building and South Africa's narrow policy agenda. *Journal of Education Policy, 6*(6), 693–716.

Christie, P. (2006). Changing regimes: Governmentality and education policy in post-apartheid South Africa. *International Journal of Educational Development, 26*, 373–381.

Christie, P., & Collins, C. (1982). Bantu education: Apartheid ideology or labour reproduction? *Comparative Education, 18*(1), 59–75.

de Clercq, F. (1997). Policy intervention and power shifts: An evaluation of South Africa's education restructuring policies. *Journal of Education Policy, 12*(3), 127–146.

Department of Education. (1997). *Curriculum 2005.* Retrieved from http://www.polity.org.za/govdocs/misc/curr2005html

Department of Education. (2002). *Revised national curriculum statement for further education and training.* Discussion document. Pretoria: Author.

Department of Basic Education. (2003). *National curriculum statement for further education and training.* Discussion document. Pretoria: Author.

Department of Basic Education. (2006). *Physical sciences national curriculum statement: Grades 10–12 (General).* Pretoria: Author.

Department of Basic Education. (2008). *National curriculum statement for further education and training.* Discussion document. Pretoria: Author.

Department of Basic Education. (2010). *Curriculum and assessment policy statement for further education and training—Physical science.* Pretoria: Author.

Enslin, P. (1984). The role of fundamental pedagogics in the formulation of education policy in South Africa. In P. Kallaway (Ed.), *Apartheid and education: The education of black South Africans* (pp. 139–147). Johannesburg: Ravan Press.

Foucault, M. (1980). Power/Knowledge. In C. Gordon (Ed.), *Selected interview and other writings* (pp. 1972–1977). Brighton: Harvester Press.

Foucault, M. (1982). The subject and power. In H. Dreyfus & P. Rainbow (Eds.), *Michel Foucault: Beyond structuralism and hermeneutics*. Chicago, IL: University of Chicago Press.

Foucault, M. (1991). Governmentality. In P. Rabinow (Ed.), *The Foucault reader: An introduction to Foucault's thought* (pp. 1–22). Harmondsworth: Penguin.

Foucault, M. (2002). Interview with Michel Foucault. In D. Faubion (Ed.), *Michelle Foucault: Power* (pp. 1–16). Harmondsworth: Penguin.

Foundation for Research and Development. (1993). South African science and technology indicators: Foundation for research and development. Pretoria: Author.

Gredley, S. (2015). Learning through experience; Making sense of students' learning through service learning. *South African Journal of Higher Education, 29*(3), 243–261.

Hodgson, N. (2010). Narrative and social justice from the perspective of governmentality. *Journal of Philosophy of Education, 43*(4), 559–572.

Honan, E. (2004). (Im)plausibities: A rhizo-textual analysis of policy text and teachers work. *Education Policy and Theory, 36*(3), 267–281.

Jansen, J. D. (2002). Political symbolism as policy craft: Explaining none reform in South African education after apartheid. *Journal of Education Policy, 17*(2), 199–215.

Jegede, O. (1999). Science education in nonwestern cultures: Towards a theory of collateral learning. In L. Semali & J. Kincheloe (Eds.), *What is indigenous knowledge? Voices from the academy* (pp. 119–142). New York: Falmer Press.

Kahn, M. (1993). Building the base: Report on a sector study of science education and mathematics education. Pretoria: Commission of the European Communities & Johannesburg: Kagiso Trust.

Kallaway, P. (2011). Science and policy: Anthropology and education in British colonial Africa during inter-war years. *PaedogicaHistorica, 1*(1), 1–20.

Koopman, O. (2013). Teachers' experiences of implementing the further education and training science curriculum. Unpublished Doctoral Dissertation, Stellenbosch University, Stellenbosch.

Le Grange, L. (2008). The history of biology as a school subject and developments in the subject in contemporary South Africa. *Southern African Review of Education, 14*(3), 89–105.

Le Grange, L. (2015). Rethinking learner-centred education: Challenges faced by the African child when learning school science and mathematics. *Journal of Educational studies, Special Issue*.

Le Grange, L., Reddy, C., & Beets, P. (2012). Socially critical education for a sustainable Stellenbosch by 2030. In M. Swilling, B. Sebitosi, & R. Loots (Eds.), *Sustainable Stellenbosch: Opening dialogues* (pp. 310–321). Stellenbosch: African Sun Media Publishers.

Naidoo, P., & Lewin, K. M. (1998). Policy and planning of Physical Science education in South Africa: Myths and realities. *Journal of Research in Science Teaching, 35*(7), 729–744.

Odora-Hoppers, C. A., & Richards, H. (2011). *Rethinking thinking.* Pretoria South Africa: Unisa Press.

Ogunniyi, M. B. (1986). Two decades of science education in Africa. *Science Education, 70*(2), 111–122.

Ogunniyi, M. B. (1988). Adapting Western science to traditional African culture. *International Journal of Science Education, 10*(1), 1–9.

Ogunniyi, M. B. (1996). Science technology and mathematics: The problem of developing critical human capital in Africa. *International Journal of Science Education, 18*(3), 267–284.

Pink, W. T. (1990). Implementing curriculum inquiry: Theoretical and practical implications. In J. T. Sears & J. J. Marshall (Eds.), *Teaching and thinking about curriculum: Critical inquiries.* New York, NY: Teachers College Press.

Simon, M. (2007). *Learning as investment: Notes on governmentality and biopolitics.* In J. Masschelein, M. Simon, U. Brockling, & L. Pongratz (Eds.), *The learning society from the perspective of governmentality.* Oxford: Blackwell.

Taylor, F. W. (1911). *The principles of scientific management.* New York: Harper and Brothers.

Thomson, A. (2002). *Critical reasoning: A practical introduction* (2 ed.). London: Routledge.

Walters, S. W. (1964). Die natuurwetenskaplik-begaafdehoërskoolleerling in die Kaapprovinsie: 'n Aspek van die problem van die onderwys van die begaafdeleerling (Unpublished master's thesis). Stellenbosch University, Stellenbosch.

Zipin, L., Fataar, A., & Brennan, M. (2015). Can social realism do social justice? Debating the warrants for curriculum knowledge selection. Education as change. doi:10.1080/16823206.2015.1085610.

Note

1. The term *Afrikaner* refers to a group of white settlers of European and Dutch descent who migrated to the southernmost tip of Africa, where they imposed colonial rule, values and culture on the indigenous populations. They also became independent and developed their own language, Afrikaans, which is claimed to be one of the fastest developing languages in the world.

CHAPTER 3

My Becoming and Unbecoming: Life as a Child, Learner and University Science Student

INTRODUCTION

This chapter was inspired by an informal conversation between me and my nine-year-old daughter who, at the time of writing, was in Grade 4. The conversation started with a simple question, 'What are things like at school?' and quickly turned into an incident for mourning when she replied, 'Fine, Daddy, but why does our history teacher's not know who Steve Biko was?' My daughter's response was cause for concern as the tone of her voice, eyes and facial expression reflected sheer disappointment in her teacher. This prompted me to probe for detail. The following dialogue between me and my daughter ensued about the life and legacy of Steve Biko, one of South Africa's greatest freedom fighters, who died from severe head injuries sustained while being interrogated by the dreaded security police.

Child: 'My teacher told us that Steve Biko died as a result of a hunger strike in prison and that he had no children and [but] the books I read and the internet say he was murdered.'

Father: 'Did you question your teacher about these facts?'

Child: 'Yes, I put up my hand and said, "Excuse me, Miss. Steve Biko was murdered and he had five children."'

Father: 'What did your teacher say when you told her this?'

O. Koopman, *Science Education and Curriculum in South Africa*,
DOI 10.1007/978-3-319-40766-1_3

Child: 'She asked me, "What do you mean with he was murdered?
            Where did you get these facts? Why do you know so much
            about Steve Biko?"'
Father: 'Tell me more about what happened next.'
Child: 'I said, "Steve Biko is one of my heroes, Miss, and he was
            beaten to death by the police and the names of his children
            were…" And our teacher said that it is not true. But I told
            her, "I have the book about his life in my bag I can show
            you, Miss." [Child then explains that she took the book out
            of her bag and started paging through it to show her teacher
            the evidence]. "Here it is, Miss, and here are the names of
            all his children."'
Teacher: 'Whoever wrote this book is wrong, and in this class I am the
            teacher and you will believe what I tell you.'
Child: 'But, Miss, this is not the only book that says these things
            about Steve Biko. I have also [re]searched it on the internet.'
Teacher: 'Keep quiet and don't backchat me.'

This conversation created a welter of emotions which veered between anger, disappointment and sadness. My anger momentarily paralysed me as the emotions flooded through my mind—I could not believe that after more than 20 years of democracy, my child was trapped in an environment which, as Madeleine Grumet (1990) points out, was designed to produce 'robots'. This incident took me back to my own journey and reminded me how some of my science teachers and lecturers ridiculed and manipulated my thinking by handing down ready-made knowledge through which they constructed the world for me. The questions that echoed through my mind were: Whose knowledge is this? Who benefits from this obscure so-called legitimate knowledge? and What can I do as a critical educator to change this and other existing educational practices? I realise that these are not only complex questions requiring complex answers but also complex questions linked to power relations.

This chapter chronicles my own lived educational experiences as a secondary-school learner and university student of science and describes my becoming—that is, the role my science teachers and university lecturers played in my personal intellectual development and growth in understanding the subject. It also dissects my unbecoming—that is, how I had to resolve the tension between the often obscure views of my science teachers and lecturers. From this perspective, I discuss what my science teachers and lecturers made me believe science was all about, and my own personal engagement with science later in life as a teacher and university lecturer in chemistry. Like in Nietzsche's Zarathustra, my narrative speaks of flux, in which the suffocating dogmatism of false and obscure notions and conceptions of science shattered against my personal engagement with the work of great scientists such as Newton and Boyle. The work of these scientists not only assisted me in acquiring a better understanding of science but also helped me to interrogate and overcome the incomprehensible views and ideas of my science teachers.

This chapter is divided into four sections. Firstly, it provides a critique of the hugely influential, all-pervasive educational doctrine of FP, which was closely aligned to the ideology of CNE at the time. Secondly, it discusses my childhood experiences in relation to the core values instilled in me as a child and its backwash effect on my intellectual development at school. Thirdly, it discusses the connection between my primary and secondary school experiences and the extent to which my teachers' subservience to the pernicious doctrine of FP influenced my thinking and attitudes towards science and shaped my understanding of the discipline. In conclusion, it explains how my growing resistance and opposition to FP and the extent to which its misgivings were consistent with the basic principles of phenomenology.

A Brief Overview of FP (Pre-1994)

The aim of this section is to give the reader a brief overview of how FP developed in South Africa and how it was used as a doctrine to create an inferior educational experience for black people. As my science teachers and university lecturers were trained in this tradition, it accounts for their mechanistic understanding of and thinking about science and how they passed the same tradition on to their learners and students. This brief background sketch will help to shed light on the essentials of FP, such as its ideological underpinnings, its autonomous approaches to the teaching and learning environment, and the interrelationship between the teacher and learner in the delivery of the curriculum content.

At the time I started attending primary school in the early eighties, FP was the official doctrine that determined the nature of instruction and learning in all schools, Afrikaans-medium universities and historically black colleges and universities. According to Le Grange (2008), the doctrine of FP, which was built on the ideology of CNE, emerged in 1944 as an instrument through which apartheid education was 'legitimised'. CNE, Enslin (1984) states, was promulgated as a policy for white Afrikaner learners, with the aim of educating black people for unequal participation in economic and social life. She states that according to CNE policy for black education, instruction should (1) be in the mother tongue, (2) not be funded at the expense of white education, (3) preserve the 'cultural identity' of the black community and (4) be administered by whites only. According to Articles 14 and 15 of the CNE policy, black education is the responsibility of white South Africa. Enslin (1984, 140) corroborates this statement when she writes,

> Bla ibility of 'white South Africa', or more specifically Of 'the Boer nation as the senior trustee of the native', who is in a state of 'cultural infancy'. A 'sub-ordinate part of the vocation and task of the Afrikaner' is to 'Christianise the non-white races of our fatherland'. It is the 'sacred obligation' of the Afrikaner to base black education on Christian National principles. Thus, revealingly, 'We believe that only when the coloured man has been Christianised can he and will he be secure against his own heathen and all kinds of foreign ideologies which promise him sham happiness, but in the long run will make him unsatisfied and unhappy'.

The juxtaposition of Christianity and pedagogy under the 'philosophy of FP' provided the justification for the authoritarian practices of teachers in South Africa under apartheid. Enslin (1990, 87) explicates,

> Central to the content of the educational doctrine endorsed by Fundamental Pedagogics, as distinct from but complementing its methodology, is the claim that education is, universally, the leading of the helpless dependent child to adulthood by the adult pedagogue. Out of this claim emerges the justification for authoritarian practices.

This justification for the authoritarian pedagogies created the opportunity to make black learners feel inferior to whites. It is also assisted in teaching the white Afrikaans-speaking child that he or she was part of a superior nation that had to seek self-determination and to live separately but at the same time Christianise the blacks "who are still in cultural infancy" (Le Grange 2008, 405). The aim of the racist CNE policy was the establishment of a separate and inferior education system for black people to ensure their unequal participation in economic and social life (Enslin 1984).

Naidoo and Lewin (1998, 732) point out that South African education was separated into schools within the Republic of South Africa and the so-called self-governing territories of Venda, Ciskei, Transkei and Bophuthatswana (which were later reincorporated into the 'new South Africa'). Within the boundaries of the Republic of South Africa, the education system was administered through four main departments: the House of Assembly (DET-A) for those classified as white, the House of Delegates (DET-D) for Indian people, the House of Representatives (DET-R) for coloured people and the DET for black people. In addition, some provinces were further subdivided into their own educational systems.

During this period, the proportion of unqualified physical science teachers employed in schools classified under the Group Areas Act of 1966 was as follows: coloured 43 %, black (Africans) 87 %, Indian 4 % and white 2 % (Naidoo and Lewin 1998). The physical science curriculum under apartheid rule was delivered to learners in an excessively theoretical and old-fashioned way (Nganu 1991). According to Kahn (1993, 8), this was as a result of a teacher-centred regime that was strict, inflexible and dominated by examinations. The syllabi were outdated. At a conference held in Johannesburg in September 1993, the ANC expressed the view that the science curriculum was trapped in a traditional and abstract paradigm, with very little attention being given to the everyday experience of learners. Too much emphasis was placed on facts and rote learning. The end result, according to the Foundation for Research and Development (1993), was that out of the entire learner population in South Africa, 47 % of white learners chose physical science when compared to 14 % of Africans, of which the average pass rate for white learners was as high as 90 % and for black learners lower than 10 %.

Krüger (2008) traces FP back to the work of B.F. Nel (1968), C.K. Oberholzer (1955 and 1968), Landman, van Zyl and Roos (1975), Van der Stoep (1969) and various others, who were all members of the faculty of education at the University of Pretoria. The first publication of FP in South Africa, *Inleiding tot die Prinsipiële Opvoedkunde* (Introduction to Fundamental Pedagogics) by C.K. Oberholzer (1954), led to FP becoming a powerful doctrine in the 1960s, 1970s and 1980s. According to Oberholzer (1968), FP is 'relatively autonomous' because it has fixed essences that disclose the structures of phenomena (170). The important task of FP is for the teacher to describe the phenomenon so accurately that it does not provide any basis for debate or argument (Landman cited in Barnard 1992). The pedagogical environment neither provides room for deeper engagement with and exploration of the meaning of the phenomenon, nor encourages any open-minded dialogue, discussion or exploration of ideas in science. Furthermore, it does not view the subject content as an opportunity to train learners to live responsibly. For example, in contemporary South Africa, the CAPS, which is underpinned by a constructivist philosophy, envisages a learner that is open-minded, critical and capable of using content to save lives. This means that when the instructor teaches Charles Law in the chemistry classroom, learners are expected to see the link between the law (i.e. an increase in pressure causes an increase in temperature) and accidents on the road. In other words, they must not only know the law but be able to apply it effectively in everyday life.

Instead, science was taught in a way that promoted only the 'fundamentals' of the content through which the broader detail and applications of the content were ignored. According to Le Grange (2008), the fundamentals had a strong theoretical focus and formed the essential framework with which the teacher approached the learning environment and the design of classroom activities. In the process, the teacher was viewed as the one that unlocked reality for the child in the form of statements without discussions or deliberations. Such FP approaches compartmentalised knowledge and promoted a behaviourist philosophy. In such a system, the child was perceived to be an empty vessel waiting to be filled, that is, the passive recipient of knowledge because of the strong emphasis on the content.

The findings of Koopman's (2013) doctoral study, which investigated the lived experiences of physical science teachers who were themselves learners in the 1970s and 1980s, corroborate the way science was taught as described in the previous paragraph. It is small wonder that the teachers expressed their disgust at the way science was thought to them. They explained how they had to learn science on their own through memorisation as their physical science teachers forced them to memorise key concepts and definitions for examinations from textbooks. One teacher pointed out that although it was his dream to become a plant pathologist, he decided to become a physical science teacher instead to help improve the way science was taught in schools. When he entered the profession, he saw his role as that of an activist who had to ensure that more learners enrolled for physical science to prevent the subject from dying out in some schools because of the absence of subject teachers. The teachers also explained the difference in content between when they were at school and what they were currently expected to teach. For example, during the 1970s and 1980s, the mechanics section (which included vectors and scalars, forces, momentum and electricity) only focussed on rectilinear motion (one dimension), which was very elementary. At university, the focus on these topics was on in two- and three-dimensional motions. This shift from one to two and three dimensions confused them because it required spatial perceptions and scientific equations that were different from those which they had been taught at school. Furthermore, solving such problems required more complicated mathematics. This dumbing down of standards they described as deliberate because motion in two dimensions formed part of the curriculum in the same standards/grades on other parts of the African continent.

My Childhood

I was born in a small suburb of Cape Town notorious for poverty, illiteracy, gangsterism and high dropout rates among school children. Cape Town can be described as a microcosm of South Africa and home to the historically so-called coloured people—people of mixed-race heritage. It is reported that, since 1671, interracial sexual contact had not been confined to white and black persons but also included the Khoikhoi. In 1781, the offspring of white and black Khoikhoi interracial mixing were classified as coloured people in the Cape as they represented more than one-sixth of the total population of Cape Town (Le Roux 2011). The promulgation of the Land Reform Act of 1913 and the Group Areas Act of 1966 saw my parents and many other 'non-white' people being forcibly removed from their birthplace to areas historically designated as coloured neighbourhoods. As a result, my parents, like many other coloured families, lived in self-constructed makeshift shelters known as shacks with no access to electricity and technology (television, computers and the internet).

During the first five years of my life, I lived (and still do) on the fringes of society where race, ethnicity, colour, socio-economic status and education intersect. I realised that I was labelled as 'coloured' in my teenage years. Although I did not understand the complexity of my race, its multilayered meanings overlapped with my identity. As a child, I was brought up to be passive and meek: respecting and not questioning my parents and my elders; it was a core value reinforced through religion. In Sunday school, we were reminded to honour our parents and never to forget to show the upmost respect and kindness to others even at the expense of our dignity. We were made to believe that the 'self' was less important than everything else. Rooted in the deep and inscrutable regions of my unconscious, my inner 'self' went into hiding most of the time. As a child I had to mask my deepest emotions and had to 'prepare a happy face to meet the faces' that I would meet as an engaging projection screen for the people around me and in the community. The key words that continually resonated in my consciousness during childhood were 'obedience', 'sub-servience', (be a) 'peacemaker', 'harmony' and 'humility', to name but a few. This 'appearance' (mask) foisted upon me represents a fraction or preformation of what society wanted me to become.

Obedience during childhood, Nietzsche (1967) argues, is not enforced to keep a child in check but to preserve the rich cultural and historical heritage of the parents. The reason parents impose this heritage on their children is to conserve the past by duplicating themselves in their children. Nietzsche (1968) argues that one's sense of right or wrong is psycho-logically induced in the subconscious mind by the strong and powerful in a society which, in my case, was my parents. These values, in turn, are predetermined by the parents. This Nietzsche calls a 'historical sickness' which attacks and shapes the essence of the child. In this manner, parents narrow the child's horizon and outlook on life, which marks the start of a constrained process of becoming in which the child is quickly trapped. Nietzsche writes, "Parents involuntarily make something like themselves out of their children—they call that education..." (1968, 194). Therefore 'parents-speak', coupled with the dismissive statement 'I say so', becomes a deplorable restriction on the creativeness and freedom with which the child looks at the world. If parents wish their children to face the world and the future bravely, creatively and without limitations, they should draw their children into the world of freedom with natural restrictions. The secret to natural restrictions, according to Rousseau (1993), is not that the child will grow up to be wild, uncontrolled or unconstraint but will learn through natural lessons of pain and frustration to adapt their desires to their abilities. Rousseau argues that nature is the master and the teacher is only the tutor on standby when needed. The child must be made to believe that he or she is learning naturally and the parent/ teacher must arrange activities carefully. He writes, "Let him [child] think he is master while you (parent) are really master" (Rousseau 1993, 100). Related to my childhood experience, 'I say so' or 'You must submit to those older than you' was a way of unconsciously inducing my conscious-ness to overcome the instinctive exercise of power over others while at the same time limiting my own growth and development. This, I realised later, had a significant backwash effect on my schooling, which my teachers used to their advantage to manipulate me. This is because it made me soft and suppressed the ability to make my thoughts known because I felt unprotected. It created the impression that I was a 'walkover' and someone that could easily be defeated.

To prevent a child from being manipulated or controlled, Socrates points out, it is essential to give shape and structure to the child in the first years of his or her young life (Kohan 2011). This is because everything that follows later in the child's life depends on those first years. In other words, a child should go through a stage of being meaningfully mirrored by significant others, usually the parents. For this reason, the Greeks devoted a considerable amount of time and energy to their children in order to give form and structure to children in whom there was no form and structure. What was of great importance to them was not so much the child, but what the child was capable of becoming. Failure to do so could reduce a child's understanding and outlook on the world. Reflecting on my childhood experiences, I realise that this was the starting point of my becoming. This phase marks the creation of metaphysical and ontologically controlled environments that shaped my thinking. It can be described as what Kant (1990) calls 'the opposition of tutelage' (83)— that is, the demands imposed on a child (or person) to become what his or her parents want him or her to become. This means that instead of acting autonomously as a child, I was forced to act heteronomously, that is, always according to the will and dictates of my parents and others and never according to my own will. This represents a revolutionary space and stage of my life that limited rather than encouraged independence and independent learning because it was misguidedly viewed as a threat to power and authority. During this phase, my natural becoming was interrupted by my parents' history from which I could not escape. In other words, the history, culture and society which are directly influenced by the economic and political factors in which I was enmeshed blocked my natural becoming. Kohan (2011) argues that, on the one hand, there are the spaces of macro-politics, of the state, where all the different institutions, with their own laws, principles and dichotomies (342) influence a society while, on the other hand, there are the micro-politics—ideologies and doctrines, with binaries and multiplicities (342). These political forces inherent in the community further restrict the child's freedom which is considered an essential part of the child's becoming (Deleuze 1991). The restriction of the child's freedom forms part of a society's disciplinary technique, which Foucault (1988, 16) calls "technologies of the self"— ways of controlling the child's thinking which determines his or her active engagement with phenomena and ways of reasoning.

My childhood can therefore be described as a collapse and reduction of my own inner 'self' in which the rich cultural history of my parents and the society I was born into dominated my thinking and outlook on life (Hoveid and Finne 2014). Seen in this way, Nietzsche (1967) avers, childhood becomes a repeat of the way a child's parents experienced the world. This implicit pressure for 'sameness' can be described as debt a child supposedly owes to his or her parents.

My Primary School Experiences

Primary school learners cherish their relationships with teachers and become excited about what excites their teachers. They are driven to impress their teachers and want to build close relationships with them. Consequently, during class time learners answer questions by focussing only on what they think their teachers want to hear. This happens because our teachers create and instil inexplicable states of consciousness characterised by fear, vilification, illogical trains of thought and other phobias into our minds. For example, learners who did not perform well in a test or could not answer questions in class or were absent from school or misbehaved or showed signs of opposition to the prevailing traditions in class and at school, such learners were flogged with a cane in class or sent to the principal's office for more severe forms of punishment. These states of consciousness crystallised in my mind and became a way of life when we entered the school gates in the mornings. When we reported and complained about these harsh forms of punishment to our parents, we were told that a teacher would not behave badly without good cause and were perversely advised to accept it as a demonstration of how much our teachers cared about and loved us.

I was formally introduced to science for the first time in Grade 3 as Nature Study. Themes such as 'Me and My Body', 'How to Cross a Road?' and 'Littering' were some of the topics in the syllabus. In Grades 4–7, the subject was called Natural Science. The content became more structured and included more life sciences topics than physical science topics—for example, the habitat, structure and morphology of selected plants and animals. *Forces* and *electricity* are the only bits of physical science (taught at an elementary level) I can remember. In every lesson, the teacher would talk for the entire period, and all the learners did was to sit passively and listen or copy notes from the blackboard. I could not see any difference between the way in which science and my other subjects were taught. For example, there was no attempt to link science to the aesthetic qualities of the open fields I played in or the rivers that flowed through our neighbourhood. In this regard, my creativity, lived-world experiences and passions were stunted. In fact, the fearsome official teaching style of our science teacher broke down our self-confidence and self-esteem. For example, the fear of asking questions, of failing, and even of talking in class were the intimidating and inhibiting norm. These values militated against any positive conception of school science and created a servile mentality devoid of personal dynamism. In the mornings when I was getting ready for school, the voice that echoed in my mind was one that reminded me how much I feared and hated my teachers and, as a result, school; consequently, I could not wait for the school day to end.

During this phase of my life, I was unconsciously drawn into the web of FP. This doctrine can be described as consisting of 'lines of power [and domination] or dualisms' that clashed with our views and experiences of how the world works and how objects in nature behave. Each power line had its own segmentation with its own objectives. One of the clashing alien objectives was the negation of the 'self' in that we had to make room in our thoughts for many useless principles, formalities and blank ideals even though they cramped our understanding of the world. In simple terms, this meant that we had to embrace that which we did not believe in, agree with what we disagreed with, and incorporate these discordant values into our way of life—hence, the nature of becoming is also the nature of change. This resulted in the establishment of new relationships which we had with ourselves, with others, with *how* and *what* we thought. It was along these lines of power and domination that new ways of thinking and doing were being imposed on us. This becoming was being foisted upon us to surrender our subjectivity as a more forceful power grew from outside to usurp our thoughts. We found ourselves in a space of non-negotiation which resulted in subservience. We did not have the power to overcome the dominating discourse of our teachers and had to surrender our freedom and accept what they taught we should learn and know.

MY HIGH SCHOOL EXPERIENCES

In high school, we only had one physical science class from Grades 10 to 12, which was restricted to 25–30 learners due to limited laboratory facilities and scarce resources. Learners were selected on the basis of their Grade-9 results. The parents of the academically excluded learners would fight with the principal to review their child's application for admission to the science class. This was because the physical science class was considered the 'cream of the crop' compared to the rest of the school and because learners who performed well in the subject had a bright future. The subject would allow them entry into careers in the field of medicine, engineering, biological science, and so forth, which was often seen as an escape from the impoverished community they were born in. I was overwhelmed when I received the news that I had been admitted to the physical science class.

At the time, there were no computers, data projectors or graphic simulations to excite our senses and to expose us to the microscopic nature and wonders of science, which is only accessible via the imagination. The only resources our teacher had were a textbook by Brink and Jones (1984), a piece of chalk and a duster. Textbook writers Bucat and Mocerino (2009), who investigated the quality of various science textbooks, found that publishers often use language imprecisely, with the result that the distinction between the macroscopic and microscopic levels is blurred rather than sharpened. The textbook by Brink and Jones lacks scientific rigour and linguistic precision. For this reason, it was disallowed in schools in the aftermath of apartheid education. Even though the school had a well-resourced laboratory with sophisticated equipment and a storeroom fully stocked with various chemicals, our teacher would spend his classroom time transmitting the official state syllabi to us verbally. The core function of his 'chalk and talk' method was to prepare us for the examination. Like our primary school teachers, and consistent with the principles of FP, he perceived us as passive recipients of knowledge who were not allowed to see, feel, touch or smell the equipment and chemicals in the laboratory. Fig. 3.1 illustrates his teaching method.

As illustrated in Fig. 3.1, the teaching of the content was confined to the core syllabus, textbooks and the examination. Our understanding of science was limited to the knowledge our teacher imparted. Most of the time when we were asked to account for our knowledge about a phenomenon, the standard response was 'because our teacher told us so'. The actual teaching included very little practical work, and no link (subject integration) was made between daily life issues and the content. In fact,

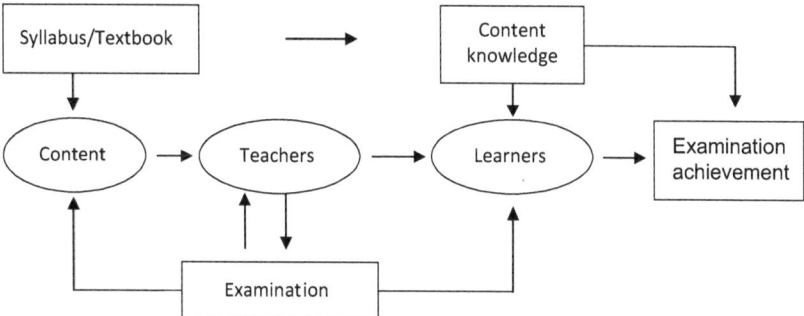

Fig. 3.1 A diagram illustrating the didactical approach of my physical science teacher

the content, learners and teachers interacted only in one way, and all of these components appeared to be related to lower-order cognitive skills. The sublime interconnectedness of science with nature and God's moral injunction for humankind to control the earth were absent. In the examinations, we were required to regurgitate the information taught to us by our teacher.

I was taught by the same teacher until I completed secondary school and discovered later that he was underqualified to teach the subject. He held a teaching certificate which he had obtained at a teacher's college. He did not have a degree in science and consequently struggled to introduce us to the processes of science to explain how eminent scientists such as Isaac Newton and Robert Boyle, to name only two, discovered the laws, principles and theories they are renowned for. As a result, the subject was little more than a dull, dry, obsolete and fragmented body of knowledge. If practical work was done at all, it was only to confirm the known; similarly, any data I collected during experiments that deviated from the textbook data were considered wrong. The only forms of assessments were class tests and examinations.

The pedagogy of my science teacher can be described as a form of dualistic Cartesian metaphysics in terms of which we were split into two essential substances, namely matter and mind. Magrini (2015, 281) avers that in such a paradigm the mind of the learner is cut off from the world and the body is reduced to matter. When this happens, the body becomes part of the mechanistic matter of the physical world, and therefore, the learner is viewed as mere matter representing an object. This metaphysical dualism between subject (teacher) and object (learner) was dominated by the teacher who disindividualised the learner in us. In this transformative process, the learners adopt the knowledge of science as delivered by their teacher and give up their own perceptual mindset and experiences of the world. This position results in the modification of the self and the way individuals think about, feel and see themselves. As they are denied the freedom to explore, infer and construct their own knowledge of the world, they think in predetermined ways and must express themselves using a particular form of knowledge commensurate with the prevailing discourse. The learner-world dialectic is distorted and results in the learners' knowledge taking on the form of the teacher's which is validated by how well the learners perform in tests and examinations. To this end, science as a 'know-how' exercise is reconfigured into a technical mechanistic and instrumental 'know this' process which the learner views as meaningless (Magrini 2015).

I had dwelled in these classrooms for most of my high school life and hoped that I would be introduced to the mysterious and fascinating world of science at university to arrive at a better understanding of science and the world. I had many questions about the world which derived from my experiences, but none of these questions was discussed in the school physical science classroom. In the next section, I discuss my lived experiences as a university student ready to take on new challenges in a vibrant and dynamic context.

University Experiences with Science

At the beginning of my first year at university, I enrolled for physics, chemistry, mathematics and zoology to be admitted to the faculty of pharmacy, dentistry or biochemistry after the completion of my first year. At the beginning of the year, I was excited and looking forward to a whole new world of science in its complex interrelationship with and contributions to humanity. This excitement slowly dissipated as there were approximately 300 students in the first-year physics and chemistry classes. Because of the large class size, some of us had to sit on the pavement steps of the lecture theatres. Being of small and slender build, I felt smothered and lost in this huge class, with many students much older and bigger than me. Another challenge I was confronted with was coming from an Afrikaans-medium school, which was also my mother tongue, to an English-medium environment. Unconsciously, in every class I had to translate every sentence from Afrikaans into English before I could make sense of what we discussed and learned in class. It felt as if I was drowning in this environment, but I had to survive as I saw a degree in science as my only ticket out of poverty. What made me lose my optimism was that the physics and chemistry lecturer, who had obviously been trained in the same FP tradition as my former school teachers, used the same teaching methods, with little consideration for the knowledge I derived from my active engagement with the real world and brought into the classroom.

As a result of my lecturer's strong FP educational training, the content was presented mainly theoretically although real-life connections were made with the world of industry which I was unfamiliar with. These real-life connections made me realise that there is huge difference between 'knowing' and 'understanding' something as it is context-dependent. Perhaps if he had used familiar examples around me that I could see, hear, touch, taste or smell, I would have learnt more because investigating existential questions empirically would have helped me to look beyond the conceptual to see the processes of science at work. This was how Lavoisier, Newton and various other pioneer scientists learned science. They would observe a phenomenon with a strong focus on its behaviour from which they could predict its accuracy to one-thousandth of a second. For example, Lavoisier's *observation* of the calcination of tin (Tn) in a sealed glass tube led to the formulation of the conservation of mass law, which initiated a revolution in chemistry. Similarly, Boyle's preoccupations with heating substances over a flame led him to observe that different substances burn with different colours, which made him realise that it is the unique chemical properties of each substance that cause it to burn with different colours. This observation and conclusion contributed to the arrangement of elements on the periodic table according to their unique colour changes. The absence of such an approach at university turned science into little more than an 'intellectual puzzle'. In consequence, I had to change my objective from wanting to understand science to passing each and every course to obtain my degree, leave the university and earn money. When I returned after a long holiday, I could only vaguely remember some of the content, and I now realise that it was knowledge that I had memorised without perceiving it to be of any value to me. Throughout my university career, the majority of my lecturers taught didactically most of the time. Instead of being fascinated by the prospect of unravelling the mysteries of the universe, as should have been the case, I experienced science to be little more than a dry list of formulas and rules with few connections made to the world of mathematics. The practical work was not much different from the theory as, essentially, all that was expected was that we would confirm the known. This cycle of events continued throughout my university science lecture theatres.

PRACTICAL WORK AT UNIVERSITY

My first experience in the huge chemistry laboratory, with its state-of-the-art equipment and with senior students walking around in their white laboratory coats, is still fresh in my mind. We were each assigned our own workstation and given an inventory to check the workstation equipment. I was afraid and embarrassed as I had not been exposed to most of the equipment during my time at high school. I 'confirmed' that everything was there without checking carefully. Afterwards, this became even more embarrassing as I was expected to work with the equipment. Once a week in the afternoon, two to three hours were devoted to chemistry and physics, respectively, practical works. I panicked every day we had to do practical work. Consequently, activities that were supposed to be challenging and enjoyable became painfully dull routines because my only motivation was to complete them successfully. The negative mindset I had towards practical work was enervating. What sometimes saved me from this intensely negative mindset, or the embarrassment of not knowing what to do, was when the laboratory technician would demonstrate the proper use of the equipment. I would feel relieved when I could submit my report, irrespective of whether it was right or wrong, as long as I could get out of the science laboratory. This negative mindset towards practical work prevailed for the most part of my university career, and I continued to fear the practical work. Most of my peers actually cancelled the subject and enrolled for other courses because their fear had turned into active hatred of the subject. They complained about struggling with incomprehensible concepts and of being made to feel like fools because they did not understand the work.

After completing my bachelor of science degree and being unable to find a suitable job as a black graduate, I decided to enrol for a one-year higher diploma in education, specialising in science. Trained in FP, I started teaching physical science at a high school in 1999 using constructivist pedagogy. For most of my eight-year long teaching career, I taught physical science at different historically disadvantaged schools with at times inadequate or no laboratory facilities and resources. Most of the learners came from broken or single-parent families, often with little or no parental support. As I was still a novice, my lessons would reflect traditional teaching methods dominated by a FP philosophy using the chalk-and-talk approach, without any consideration for the learner's worldviews and real-world experiences. Furthermore, my lessons were mostly directed at preparing learners for examinations as I was weighed down by the testing regime, policies and other requirements for conformity and compliance of the Department of Basic Education. My teaching approaches were framed by what Spiegelberg (1960) describes as one's historical roots and consciousness (FP) reaching out. My historical roots and consciousness were the ways in which I was taught and trained as a learner of physical science. Cohen (1990) argues that I was trapped in FP and reproducing my old ways of learning. He points out that teachers often have difficulty adjusting their old ideas, beliefs, practices and ways of doing things. My teaching approach became a psychological preference, which I needed to unlearn.

My Unbecoming

Becoming Critical

The question that constantly echoed in my mind was: 'How do I move from theoretical critique to action that will bring about the desired change?' From Habermas (1972) I learned that all knowledge is produced by the ways people orient themselves to the world. Although Habermas identifies three basic orientations, each governed by a particular interest, I want to focus on two of the three orientations that influenced my thinking and subsequently assisted me in changing my orientation towards the teaching and learning of science. Firstly, Habermas (1972) stresses the crucial role of communication in the construction of knowledge. According to Habermas, communication is governed by a practical interest in understanding others. The type of knowledge generated from this perspective is situational and interpretive rather than generalisable and empirical. It assisted me in showing greater appreciation for who my learners were and the knowledge they brought into the science classroom. I realised that each learner was different, had different experiences, had different outlooks on the world and learned differently. The second orientation to knowledge, according to Habermas, is freedom. It is centred on an emancipatory interest in liberating individuals from oppressive environments which, in turn, produce critically reflective knowledge. I realised that these orientations to knowledge espoused by Habermas pervaded my training as a learner and university student and that the focus was more on the technical orientation to knowledge where I was treated like an object instead of a subjective epistemological being in control of my own environment and destiny. I realised that what was needed to root out the dominating tradition of FP and to move to action was a continuous critical reflective discourse.

The main challenge in maintaining my momentum in breaking with the tradition of FP was the sheer weight and pressure of the state policies and prescribed practices. It rendered escaping from this mindset extremely difficult as the dominating systems of power quickly forced me back into my old habits and ideas. My desire to escape from the safe and comfortable 'chalk and talk' method never stopped, and this drive assisted me in fighting the natural flow of life. I kept on saying to myself that things had to change if I wanted to produce independent thinkers that were passionate about science. To create independent thinkers, I needed to shift my lessons from a world of facts and appearances that lacked scientificity to an intelligible world of thinking where my learners could embark on a personal voyage of discovery and enlightenment. These realisations unsettled and threatened my old ways of being and existing. My troubled state of mind and my misgivings about the prevailing philosophy of FP marked the starting point of my unbecoming. The philosophy that lay at the heart of this process was phenomenology. It was phenomenological not because of some kind of method I was using but because of constant reflection and dissection of what was happening in my classrooms. I reflected daily on the content and structure of my thoughts and on the experiences of my learners and how they struggled with the content and realised that I had to give up the ideological child of FP. This process of constant reflection taught me a great deal about myself and made me realise how conditioned I was and that the mental residues imprinted on my subconscious mind lacked scientificity. As I connected with a deeper and more real self, it dawned on me that in order for my learners to see and feel what scientists see, I had to allow them to explore, infer and hypothesise so that they could learn to know on their own what scientists know. In other words, I wanted to expose my learners to real science and not to a pseudo-image of science.

The Phenomenological Method

In a phenomenological paradigm the focus is not on the learning of facts but in discovering the ultimate truths about the universe through personal experience. From Heidegger I learned that the nature of our existence is not cognitive but concrete in the sense that it involves real beings who are physically present in the world and whose knowledge of the world is derived from their personal interaction with 'concrete physical things' in their immediate lifeworld (1967, p. 58). These visible and concrete physical things are experienced through our senses. An example at this point might be of assistance. If two learners are exposed to the same pictures and images of the planet Jupiter in the science classroom and two days later are asked to conjure up a thought about the Jupiter, chances are that the first thought about for both learners will be similar. This is because both learners have no concrete physical experience or a physical connection with the planet. Apart from conjuring up images of Jupiter, the exercise does not require them to use their senses, and therefore, they cannot think further than the information and instruction which the teacher has given. What both learners' thought patterns have in common is not empirical and causal content but ideal theoretical content independent of the senses. It is reasonable then to infer that any follow-up question relating to Jupiter will be beyond their reach and can be described as a 'woeful blindness' with respect to what a real image of Jupiter looks like. This example relates to the valuable role that the senses could play in the meaning-making process through which a teacher could promote learning.

Using Heidegger's (1967) philosophy of perceptual experience and by drawing on their lived experiences in most lessons, I encouraged my learners to use their senses to classify objects according to their colour, shape, structure, mass, length, and so forth. This identification of objects, which requires the effective application of the senses, became the data with which they had to frame their ideas. By experiencing different objects, challenges, stimuli or making observations, learners learn to construct their own ideas about how they think objects might behave in the surrounding real world. These predictions allow them to generate data to formulate or falsify hypotheses. The reasons for the conclusions they arrived at in an attempt to explain the way objects behave were the starting point for introducing them to how scientists work in the laboratory. These carefully guided initial steps assisted the learners in using their senses to work through these events progressively to generate meaning and understanding. At times I used statements and questions such as, 'Why can't a person see around a corner? Today the sky looks a bit bluer than yesterday' or 'What did you have for breakfast this morning?' or questions related to the forces of nature such as the colours of flowers or the colour of the ocean. I started with these questions so that the learners could use their lived experiences and senses carefully as 'scientific instruments' to dissect ontological clues and link the empirical with the aesthetic nature of things.

I witnessed that when the teaching of science is based on what children actually see when observing a phenomenon, the experience becomes easily assimilated into their memory because the external manifestations or empirical data of the phenomenon become their perceptual mindset. Although children observing such an event may not be familiar with the theory underpinning the phenomenon, it has the potential to transport them beyond the narrow bounds of what they have observed. This encourages them to start asking deeper questions, which might prompt them to conduct further investigations. Unfortunately, most textbooks use language carelessly and narrowly when explaining terms. For example, when we were given the melting points of different objects or materials, I believed that at those specified temperatures the atoms of the different substances melt and turn into liquid. This misconception was fixed in my memory for many years, and it was only much later in life that I realised that it is the intermolecular bonds that break down and that the authentic nature of the atoms remains the same. This misconception arose because most textbooks did not explain the process. If this process was described clearly in textbooks, the knowledge gained at the submicro level would not only become part of a deeper way of seeing but of a way of understanding the intra-molecular (i.e. those aspects concerned with what happen *within* molecules) and intermolecular (i.e. those concerned with the relationships *between* molecules) world. For example, by allowing the learners to bring tennis balls, bricks and various other objects into the classroom, I encouraged the class to cut or break down the objects into smaller pieces and to compare the molecular structures of the respective objects. To bring the learners even closer to the submicro level, I used different visual aids so that they could see a formula and the molecular structure or diagrams of molecules, after which I encouraged them to visualise them instead of focussing on the symbolism of molecules. From this point onwards, I encouraged them to build models of what they thought was happening inside the objects and how objects are constructed at submicro level. This was a very demanding phase of my life and a lot of hard work went into every lesson. This meant that I had to work through many different text-books and internet sources and even consult with experts to prepare for my lessons. Furthermore, I also took a keen interest and was involved in the everyday after-school life activities of my learners. For example, some Saturdays a number of learners would come over to my house to help me in the garden. During these activities we would exchange ideas about what worked and what did not work in my lesson. This also helped me to shape the context of my lesson so that I could use real-life experiences to which they could relate. This helped me with my planning as my aim was to stimulate interest in science in areas that they liked and enjoyed.

According to Husserl (1970), all learning begins and ends with experience. This is because the perceptual information or mental residues in the memory carry information about the phenomena which are linked to a particular sensory modality. This information is funnelled into two possible streams: a *responsive stream* and an *unresponsive stream*. Both of these streams can be stimulated through insightful questioning to lead the learner to a deeper understanding of the scientific phenomenon. Drawing on a learner's lived experience automatically activates the responsive stream, which leads to a deeper understanding of the phenomenon as the learner becomes more deeply aware of his or her surroundings. Science provides a rich insight into developing a closer interaction between the learner and his or her immediate environment. It is therefore important to work from an appropriate phenomenon that opens up the responsive stream to introduce the science because if the stimulus (experience) falls outside the receptor field, the 'neurons' short-circuit, leading to meaninglessness or pointless memorisation, so to speak.

Conclusion

This chapter has shown that there are strong links between a learner's intellectual development and growth and the way he or she is taught. Building on this premise, the researcher has argued that his teachers' 'fundamental' and 'elementary' approaches to the way science was taught suppressed his imagination and the desire to experiment which is needed to stimulate creativity. From this we learn that knowledge is only effective and valuable if it is interpreted through a lived experiential lens. To this end, the chapter censures the toxic doctrine of FP by arguing that the author's teachers and university lecturers reduced the processes of science to some small, intellectual tradition in which there was no relation between theory and practice. The author describes his teacher's practices as a dispassionate fundamentum. Teachers and lecturers are often guilty of unconsciously imposing state policies and practices that stunt the growth of their learners and students, which could be one of the causes of the high dropout rates in the subject. From an epistemic discourse, with regard to the author's becoming, I want to raise two key points: firstly, traditional agendas and practices not only affect learner performance and achievement but also affect literacy, which has a direct bearing on a learner's disposition towards nature and his or her immediate environment. Secondly, everyday educational lived-experience discourse, as in the author's case, could be beneficial and might be the answer to revivifying the current state of affairs of science. The end result and focus of a teacher is to enhance teaching and learning in science.

From the author's unbecoming we learn that in order to escape from dominant discourses in our lives, we need to confront the nature and structure of the prevailing traditions and practices through critical reflective discourse. Nietzsche (1967) holds that it is doctrine that affirms the antithesis and it is doctrine that rejects the antithesis. In other words, teachers are the affirmers of what is acceptable and what is not acceptable practice for the sake of and well-being of the child. Nietzsche continues by reminding us that it is not enough to be a swordsman but one must also know against whom to be a swordsman. In other words, we need to know 'who' or 'what' the dogmatisers are that shape and give meaning to our lives and find means and ways to escape from them—that is, from the nature and structure of the dominant ideology. From this perspective, the author discussed how he had to reconfigure his knowledge of science that led him to a different pathway of becoming. From the author's unbecoming we learn that becoming is always fluid because we never arrive at a final destiny.

I find it fitting to close with the story of Socrates in *The Apology* (cited by Kohan 2011) on trial for allegedly perverting the minds of young people. Socrates offers the explanation that his execution will mean the death of an innocent man because those who have learned with him will continue to do so even after he is executed. Socrates affirms what Kohan (2011, 351) calls a 'pedagogical scandal', which is the idea that a relational space exists between teacher and learner in which the learner learns without the teacher. What Socrates points out in his apology is that there is neither any causality nor directionality in this pedagogical space. In Socrates' view, his students are learning without him teaching. Furthermore, Kohan argues that the student learns, but not the knowledge delivered to him by his or her teacher. The Apology refers to a pedagogical dogma that holds that what a student learns is in the teacher and is somehow transmitted or made to appear to the learner through the specific behaviour or disposition of the teacher.

This story by Socrates, when analysed, speaks of a form of emancipation and enlightenment that empowers the learner. What is needed in the science classroom today is for teachers to teach with open-mindedness free from the objectives and outcomes predetermined by the state so that learners can develop their own rules and theories in the chemistry laboratory based on their experiences with phenomena. Socrates takes up a position within the teaching and learning environment that places his students on the same intellectual level as himself and which allows them the freedom to explore. In so doing, he creates a hunger for understanding in his students that far exceeds knowledge. It is the ignorance of the child and not the knowledge to be imparted that, Kohan (2011) argues, should be used as a context for teaching. This creates a pedagogical space that does not place boundaries or limits on the intellectual development of the learner but creates opportunities for thinking, and where facts and preconceived knowledge are relegated to a lower level than the act of experiencing science.

REFERENCES

Barnard, F. (1992). The significance of philosophy for the student of fundamental pedagogics. *South African Journal of Higher Education, 6*(1), 7–16.

Brink, B., & Jones, R. C. (1984). *Natuur-en-Skeikunde: Standard 10.* Cape Town: Juta en Kie.

Bucat, B., & Mocerino, M. (2009). Learning at the submicro level: Structural representations. In J. K. Gilbert & D. Treagust (Eds.), *Multiple representations in Chemical education.* London: Springer Science Business Media.

Cohen, D. (1990). A revolution in one classroom: The case of Mrs. Oblier's. *Educational Evaluation and Policy Analysis., 12*(3), 327–345.

Deleuze, G. (1991). Empiricism and subjectivity. New York: Columbia University Press.

Enslin, P. (1984). The role of fundamental pedagogics in the formulation of education policy in South Africa. In P. Kallaway (Ed.), *Apartheid and education: The education of black South Africans* (pp. 139–147). Johannesburg: Ravan Press.

Enslin, P. (1990). Science and doctrine: Theoretical discourse in African teacher education. In M. Nkomo (Ed.), *Pedagogy of domination* (pp. 77–92). Trenton, NJ: Africa World Press Inc.

Foucault, M. (1988). Technologies of the self. In L. Martin, H. Gutman & P. Hutton (eds.). *Technologies of the self* (pp. 16–49). Amherst: University of Massachusetts.

Foundation for Research and Development. (1993). South African science and technology indicators: Foundation for research and development. Pretoria.

Grumet, M. (1990). Existential and phenomenological foundations of autobiographical methods. In W. Pinar & W. Reynalds (Eds.), *Understanding curriculum as phenomenological and deconstructed text* (pp. 28–43). New York: Teachers College Press.

Habermas, J. (1972). *Knowledge and human interest* (J. Shapiro, Trans.). Boston: Beacon.

Heidegger, M. (1967). *Being and time* (Macquarrie, J., & Robinson, E., Trans.). SCM Press, London.

Hoveid, M. H., & Finne, A. (2014). You have to give of yourself: Care and love in pedagogical relations. *Journal of Philosophy of Education, 48*(2), 246–261.

Husserl. E. (1970). The crisis of the european sciences and transcendental phenomenology: An introduction to phenomenological philosophy (D. Carr Transl.). Evanston IL: North Western Unversity Press.

Kahn, M. (1993). Building the base: Report on a sector study of science education and mathematics education. A product of great consultation carried out for the Commission of the European Communities, Pretoria and Kagiso Trust, Johannesburg, South Africa.

Kant, I. (1990). Foundations of the metaphysics of morals and what is enlightenment? (L. Beck Transl.). New York: Macmillan.

Kohan, W. O. (2011). Childhood, education and philosophy: Notes on detrritorialisation. *Journal of Philosophy of Education, 45*(2), 339–359.

Koopman, O. (2013). Teachers' experiences at implementing the Further Education and Training science curriculum. An unpublished doctoral thesis. Stellenbosch University. Stellenbosch.

Krüger, R. A. (2008). The significance of the concepts 'elemental' and 'fundamental' in didactic theory and practise. *Journal of Curriculum Studies, 40*(2), 215–250.

Landman, W. A., van Zyl, M. E., and Roos, S. G. (1975). *Fundamenteel-pedagogiese essensies: Hulleverskyning, verwerkliking en inhougewig* [Fundamental pedagogical essences: Their appearance, actualization and giving them content]. Durban, South Africa: Butterworth.

Le Grange, L. (2008). The didactics tradition in South Africa: A reply to Richard Krüger. *Journal of Curriculum Studies, 40*(2), 399–407.

Le Roux, C. S. (2011). European foundations shaping schooling in South Africa: Early Dutch and British colonial influence at the Cape. In J. J. Booyse, C. S. Le Roux, J. Seroto, & C. C. Wolhunter (Eds.), *A history of schooling in South Africa*. Pretoria: Van Schaick Publishers.

Magrini, J. M. (2015). Phenomenology and curriculum implementation: Discerning a living curriculum through the analysis of Ted Aoki's situational praxis. *Journal of Curriculum Studies, 47*(2), 274–299.

Naidoo, P., & Lewin, K. M. (1998). Policy and planning of Physical Science education in South Africa: Myths and realities. *Journal of Research in Science Teaching, 35*(7), 729–744.

Nel, B. F. (1968). *Fundamentele orienteering in die psigologiese pedagogiek* [Fundamental orientation in psychological pedagogics]. Stellenbosch, South Africa: University Publishers and Booksellers.

Nganu, M. (1991). *Overview of African countries' strategies in tackling problems of science, technology and mathematics education in human resource development for the post-apartheid South Africa*. London, UK: Commonwealth secretariat.

Nietzsche, F. (1967). Beyond good and evil. (W. Kaufmann, Trans.). *The basic writings of Nietzsche*. New York: Random house.

Nietzsche, F. (1968). *The will to power* (W. Kaufmann & R. J. Hollingdale, Trans.). New York: Vintage Books.

Oberholzer, F. (1954). Inleiding in die prinsipiele opvoedkunde [Introduction to the principles of education]. Pretoria: Moreau.

Oberholzer, F. (1955). The toeretiese onderbou van en praktiese toepassing uit die pedagogiek [The theoretical foundation and practical application from the pedagogical]. Pretoria: Van Schaik.

Oberholzer, C. K. (1968). *Prolegomena van 'n prinsipiële pedagogiek*. HAUM: Kaapstad.

Rousseau, J. J. (1993). *Emile*. Vermont: Everyman.

Spiegelberg, H. (1960). *The phenomenological movement: A historical introduction* (2 ed.). Netherlands, Nijhoff: The Hague.

Van der Stoep, F. (1969). *Didaktiese grondvorme* [Didactic ground forms]. Pretoria: H & R Academia.

CHAPTER 4

I Am Ready for This New Curriculum: The Lived Experiences of a Physical Science Teacher

INTRODUCTION

The phenomenological investigation recounted in this chapter focuses on the *lived experiences* of a black physical science teacher who teaches in a so-called informal settlement in the Western Cape Province of South Africa. For the most part, people in informal settlements live in self-constructed makeshift shelters known as *shacks*. These dwellings are built in such close proximity to one another that they form severely congested settlements often associated with serious health and social problems. The establishment of informal settlements was the result of the racist 1913 Land Act, which relegated black South Africans to so-called native reserves; the notorious 'Group Areas Act' of 1966, which forced South Africans to live in designated areas based on racial classification and rapid urbanisation as large number of people migrated to the cities in search of better economic opportunities. The learners whom Thobani teaches physical science live in such an informal settlement township community (see Fig. 4.1).

In South Africa, a large number of studies focus on the implementation of a new science curriculum (see Aldous 2004; Jansen 1999; McDonald and Rogan 1988; Rogan and Grayson 2003 and many others). Rogan and Grayson (2003) have attempted to develop a theoretical model for curriculum implementation in developing countries based on the following aspects to minimise the waste of resources and demoralising experiences of teachers: a profile of implementation, the capacity to innovate and support

© The Author(s) 2017
O. Koopman, *Science Education and Curriculum in South Africa*,
DOI 10.1007/978-3-319-40766-1_4

Fig. 4.1 The community in which Thobani teaches

structures. Rogan (2004) examined the challenges that a new science curriculum might pose for science teachers and how well they cope with the
implementation process and concluded that without continuous support
and professional development, the process is most likely to fail. In a similar study, Kriek and Basson (2008) found that although teachers were
positive about the new curriculum, they had concerns about the lack of
resources and their ability to teach the curriculum content. This is congruent with the views of Brodie et al. (2002), who argue that teacher qualifications, specialised subject knowledge access to resources and support
structures in schools are determining factors in how teachers respond to a
new curriculum. Aldous' (2004) study looked at the factors that influence
teachers' perceptions but does not delve deep enough into the mindsets of
teachers to explain their thinking or the rationalisation undergirding their
perceptions when confronted with curriculum change.

These studies are of great value because they provide answers to specific questions of curriculum implementation. Researching teachers' lived
experiences of the implementation of a new curriculum could add to this
growing body of work and provide answers to the question why teachers
do what they do. In the last two decades, both internationally and nationally, in South Africa, there has been a significant upsurge in researching the
lived experiences of science teachers phenomenologically (e.g. see Hammer
1995; Domert et al. 2007; Clarke and Linder 2006; Koopman 2013). For
example, Clarke and Linder's (2006) study reports on the lived experiences

of a black female teacher who teaches in an informal settlement in a large, overcrowded and underresourced school and her struggle to implement the outcomes-based curriculum. Although these studies reflect a broad phenomenological approach, they do not follow through with a detailed phenomenological analysis of the data. Therefore, the research on which this study is based aimed to use not only a phenomenological data-collection process but Husserlian phenomenology to represent the findings from a genealogical angle and Heideggerian phenomenology to represent them from a portraiture angle. The next section of the study discusses the curriculum which Thobani had to implement.

The Shift to the FET NCS

In March 1997, under the rubric of C2005, indicating the final year of implementation in all school grades, the South African Department of Education (DoE 1997) launched its first post-apartheid curriculum. It was envisaged that this new curriculum would replace content-based education with outcomes-based education (OBE) and teacher-centred pedagogies with learner-centred pedagogies. Furthermore, OBE was intended to redress the legacy of apartheid by promoting the development of skills throughout the school-leaving population so as to prepare South Africa's workforce for participation in an increasingly competitive global economy.

Since the gradual phasing in of the new curriculum, it has undergone extensive revision, following a period of vociferous debate and fierce contestation as to the merits of OBE (e.g. see Jansen and Christie 1999). One of the major changes that took place with the introduction of the NCS for physical science was a shift in the subject content prescribed. For the first time, topics such as two-dimensional motion and two-dimensional momentum were included in the Mechanics section. Furthermore, other new materials in the physics section included lasers, the Doppler Effect, two- and three-dimensional waves, electrodynamics, electronics, the mechanical properties of light and electromagnetic radiation. In the chemistry section, there were few changes to the previous curriculum, but the topics were more detailed and extensively elaborated upon. The NCS aims to produce a learner who can think logically, analytically, holistically and factually (DoE 2006a, 2008). Furthermore, teachers are expected to be designers of learning programmes and materials, researchers and subject specialists (see DoE 2003).

At the time of the research reported on in this study, the NCS was the only legal curriculum document for teachers. Thobani and all the other physical science teachers were expected to fulfil the requirements of the NCS. In the NCS policy for physical science, each learning outcome (LO) was accompanied by ASs which describe the ways in which learners should attain these outcomes. According to the NCS policy document (DoE 2003), ASs are vehicles of knowledge, skills and values through which the LOs are addressed. Table 4.1 represents the three LOs and selected ASs to shed light on how physical science was structured in the NCS curriculum. This table will be used as frame of reference to describe Thobani's understanding and interpretation of the NCS in the findings and discussion section.

The LOs for Grades 10–12 are the same, but the ASs differ across grades, serving to indicate the level at which the LOs must be achieved in each grade. For example, in Grades 10 to 11 (for LO1), a learner is expected to conduct a scientific investigation and collect data for interpretation. In Grade 12, the learner must design and conduct an experiment to collect data from which to draw inferences and interpret the data to verify or falsify a particular hypothesis. The attainment of these skills (LO1) is evident when a learner uses scientific reasoning to explain the verification or falsification of his or her hypothesis. Learning outcome 2 focuses on the construction of scientific knowledge, whereas a Grade-10 learner is only expected to state the basic prescribed scientific knowledge (DoE 2003). In Grades 11 to 12, learners must define and discuss the basic prescribed

Table 4.1 Assessment standards for physical science for the respective LOs in the FET phase

	Learning Outcome 1: Scientific inquiry and problem-solving (LO 1)	Learning Outcome 2: Construction of scientific knowledge (LO 2)	Learning Outcome 3: The nature of science and its relationship to technology, society and environment (LO 3)
ASs	Planning and conducting an investigation	Recalling and stating concepts	Integrating science with technology and mathematics
	Accurate and reliable collection of data	Explaining interrelationships between facts and concepts	Impact of science on ethical and moral arguments
	Interpreting data and seeking patterns and trends	Applying scientific knowledge	Impact of science on the environment and social development

(Constructed from DoE Policy Document 2003)

scientific knowledge. Each of the concepts builds upon the previous one, from one grade to the next, which is consistent with the goal of conceptual progression. Bennet (2002, 83) points out that conceptual progression is desirable in a curriculum "as it represents elements of curriculum implementation and delivery that are crucial in synchronising policy, teaching, assessment and learning". Thus, as learners progress through the FET phase, their knowledge of scientific concepts is strengthened. The role of the NCS teacher is illustrated by way of an example below.

When teaching Boyle's Law, the teacher must not merely guide the learners to collect data to verify textbook information as in the former apartheid curriculum. Instead, the teacher now has to develop the learners' insight into the objectives and rationale behind these experiments by guiding them to understand what led Boyle to arrive at these laws. It follows that the teacher needs to be familiar with the work of Torricelli, his experimental evidence for atmospheric pressure and his design of the barometer from which Boyle derived his theories. Furthermore, it is expected of Thobani and his colleagues to encourage their learners to develop practical skills in the science classroom by allowing them to design their own experiments and collect similar data that will confirm the inverse proportionality relationship between volume and pressure if the temperature remains constant. The learners are then expected to link Boyle's Law to real life applications such as in the tyre industry where tyres with stronger casings reduce road accidents. In addition, the teacher must promote higher order cognitive skills in the learners in order for them to understand that an increase in temperature results in an increase in pressure; therefore, a stronger tyre casing would reduce the number of road accidents caused by tyre bursts.

The NCS in the FET band is based on three LOs: skill, knowledge and application. Each outcome has three ASs, except for LO 1 which has four (for full details on the NCS for physical science, see Nakedi et al. 2012). The goals of the NCS not only require teachers to use innovative teaching strategies but also expand their knowledge and perceptions about how they think learners learn. Next, the epistemic and ontological nature of the study will be discussed in order to shed light on Thobani's lived world.

PHENOMENOLOGISTS AS WORKERS OF EXPERIENCE

According to Husserl (1975, 5), cognition begins and ends with experience. Gadamer (1975, 34) argues that experience has a condensing and intensifying meaning. He maintains that the totality of experience is found in the significant whole. This significant whole refers not only to a person's presence but to his or her complete presence. Husserl (1975, xiv) notes that this whole or unity of an object is something that is given among various appearances and not something separate and alongside it. It is considered a structural nexus that is contextually connected to reflect upon so as to give it a significant quality of meaning. Therefore, according to Husserl, phenomenology is a form of inquiry that describes the lived experiences of others and informs us about the participant's perception of a physical object. These perceptions provide phenomenological researchers with the necessary intellectual tools to understand human behaviour and actions and to do something about the latter when necessary.

It is widely acknowledged in the philosophical literature that lived experience is best captured using a phenomenological framework. The phenomenological school is divided into two groups whose philosophical orientations derive from the work of the German philosophers Husserl (1859–1938) and Heidegger (1889–1976), respectively. Both groups of scholars concentrate their research activities on the idea of the lived experience. Although both groups are located within the phenomenological tradition of researching lived experience, there are marked differences between them. Husserl's (1975) pursuit of truth about human existence focuses on the theoretical and philosophical aspects of people's experience, with the emphasis on *bracketing* and *essences*. Husserl (1975) tirelessly pointed out that, in essence, phenomenology is a pure science of consciousness or a science of pure phenomena that are absolute and unique. By contrast, Heidegger (1967, 2002) focuses more on the ontological dimension and contextualisation of experience. The difference between the approaches of the mentioned scholars will become evident later in the chapter when in Husserlian terms the experiences of Thobani are narrated through use of his own words without any interpretation and then followed by a Heideggerian approach whereby Thobani's experiences are interpreted by the authors based on contextual factors. Both traditions use lived experience to elucidate and validate the manner in which people experience particular phenomena through observation and interaction, which leads them to indubitable meanings of truth about individuals. Both these traditions informed this study.

Husserl (1975) argues that lived experience (*Erlebnis*) is to be understood as first-person data, also referred to as *eidetic data* (representing the ideas of the individual). This means that first-person data are prior to any reflection given experientially to someone. Husserl (1975, xix) explains the first-person data as follows: "We must not make assertions about that which we do not see ourselves." He points out that such first-person data are synonymous with the meaning of the German word *Sachen*, which in context does not refer to physical objects but to subconsciously held ideas. These subconsciously held ideas have their roots in experience which, in our lives, refers to those matters that we value most. According to Husserl (1975, xix), the only way to access these subconsciously held ideas or structures of knowledge is through a consciousness unburdened by preconceived ideas or notions derived from the individual's personal experiences or perceptions. According to Koesterbam (in Husserl 1975, xxii), this approach generates pure presentations or uninterrupted sense data derived from experience. Husserl firmly believes that an individual's consciousness is reflected in his or her presence in the world, which represents his or her intentionality—that is, the directedness of his or her consciousness towards the object of thought. Based on this premise, the implementation of the NCS becomes not only a description of how the teacher attempts to implement the curriculum but also a description of how the process of implementation unfolds in his or her consciousness. Brown (1992, 49) sums up the latter when he writes,

> We want to understand man (sic) from his world, that is, from the meaningful ground structure of that totality of situations, events, cultural values, to which he orients himself, about which he has consciousness, and to which his actions, thoughts and feelings are related.

The above quotation expresses the main aim of the research reported to in this chapter, which was to delve into Thobani's consciousness to gather as much rich descriptive data as possible to capture his thoughts. In the next section, the attention shifts to the methodological orientations of the study.

THE RESEARCH APPROACH

This research on which this study is based was situated within a phenomenological methodological framework. Such a framework is specific because it illuminates the research subject's contextualised experiences—in this instance, the mental and emotional turbulence he experienced in response to the challenge of introducing a new physical science syllabus and to bring about renewal within his constrained teaching environment in an impoverished community. This study goes beyond the physical experiences of external events and aims to focus on the inner landscape of why he embraces or resists elements of curriculum change.

The essential interest is in exploring the objects of experience in Thobani's consciousness in order to gain deeper insight into the lifeworld of a physical science teacher as revealed through his personal accounts. Husserl (1970) stresses the importance of discovering truth by understanding the human lived experience and exploring it systematically through rigorous inquiry or research. Van Manen (1984, 38) writes,

> As we research the possible meaning structures of our lived experiences, we come to a fuller grasp of what it means to be in the world as a man, a woman, a child, taking into account the socio-cultural and the historical traditions which have given meaning to our ways of being in the world.

In phenomenology, interviews and field notes are regarded as trustworthy and reliable forms of data construction. Given the heavy workloads and administrative responsibilities of teachers, a semi-structured, in-depth, one-on-one interview—rather than an alternative form of data construction such as a descriptive essay—was used.

THE INTERVIEW

The interview questions were aligned with the main aim of the research study—which was to delve into Thobani's consciousness to gather as much rich descriptive data as possible about his thoughts and feelings concerning the implementation of the NCS—and were all framed around his experiences in this regard. The in-depth interview focussed attention on issues such as his feelings, beliefs and perceptions as regards the challenges associated with the NCS. The interview commenced with knowledge questions about his experiences as a learner, specifically with reference to the school he had attended and the physical science teacher he had had as a learner in Grade 12. This was followed with questions about how he had experienced the introduction of the NCS and the training he had received prior to the implementation, how he felt and what he thought about the NCS. Husserl's (1975, xix) principles of the phenomenological *epoché*[1] and his dictum about *the things themselves*[2] were adhered to during the data-gathering process as explained in the following paragraph.

During the interview, the researcher paid close attention to the verbal and non-verbal behaviour of the research subject by drawing on the resources of speech act theory, discourse analysis and communication science. Here, the focus was on the length of the pauses during and between questions, the interviewee's posture and gestures during the interview, and word choices. During this phase of the recorded interview, notes were made as comprehensively as possible without any bias or judgemental evaluation. The notes that were made included the non-verbal cues, silences, word choices and the repetition of certain words during the responses. The researchers also compiled a list of significant words used by the interviewee. For example, high-frequency responses such 'yo' and 'phew', and so forth, were given attention to as the interviewee tried to give emotional expression in some instances. These notes were carefully taken so that the researchers could correlate them with specific questions and responses constructed from the data (Miles and Huberman 1984).

DATA EXPLICITATION

Data explicitation is divided into two sections, namely findings and discussion. Under *findings*, we provide a descriptive narrative using mostly Thobani's direct words, comments and expressions as is customary in a phenomenological study. In the *discussion* section, we present an interpretive narrative in order to give meaning to or elucidate his direct words and to separate the essential aspects from the peripheral. Thobani's transcript was analysed by grouping together related items and responses in an attempt to arrive at an understanding of the language he used as based on his *choice* of words. At this stage, the researchers tried, as Husserl (1975) suggests, placing themselves in Thobani's position in an attempt to understand what he meant and intended to say during the interview. His responses were transformed into 'psychological language'[3]—that is, interpreted and rendered psychologically—with an emphasis on how he experienced the NCS in his consciousness. We found these transformations necessary because such psychological renderings provide a deeper insight into his responses to the events that took place in his life as a child and later as a teacher.

FINDINGS

During the data explicitation process, the researcher had to enter a totally presuppositionless space by suspending all possible interpretations and meaning. It required from the researcher to read the transcript with openness and had to enter Thobani's world in order to extract meaning from what he was saying. It must be stated that at times this was difficult because each individual (e.g. Thobani) has his/her own unique way of experiencing temporality, spatiality and materiality in this world (Hycner 1985, 29). Furthermore, to understand others in relation to their own inner world is even more complex, but the researcher connected his own experiences as an ex-learner and ex-teacher of physical science to give meaning to Thobani's lived world. In presenting the findings, he grouped the items reflecting similar responses together and identified the following themes:

1. Thobani's views on the shift from C2005 to the NCS;
2. Thobani's classroom experience and understanding (interpretation) of the NCS;
3. Thobani's responses to the training offered by the Western Cape Education Department (WCED) in preparation for the implementation of the NCS.

Before presenting the findings of Thobani's responses to the above themes, he wishes to provide a short biography of his life as a child and learner of physical science. His biography was compiled by meticulously scrutinising each word, phrase, sentence and paragraph in the interview transcripts in order to distil the essence of his childhood experiences. The first part of the interview allowed him entry into Thobani's consciousness of how he experienced the world as a child in the physical science classroom and how he ended up in the teaching profession. These experiences provided tangible structures to reconstruct his history and subsequently his biography.

GENEALOGICAL ANGLE: THOBANI'S BIOGRAPHY

At the time of the interview, Thobani was 38 years old, had been teaching physical science at school for 13 years, held a three-year Technikon (now called University of Technology) teaching diploma and was attempting to complete his fourth year to upgrade his qualification to a bachelor's degree. He was born and raised in an informal settlement in the Western Cape Province. Thobani describes the school he attended as a learner as a bare concrete building on a piece of open land which he characterised as 'a resource-poor environment' (see Fig. 4.2). In addition, he characterises his experience of the subject physical science at school as a horrible and challenging ordeal. He states, 'We (learners) never understood our teacher...I think we taught ourselves the Grade 12 syllabus.' He sardonically remarks

Fig. 4.2 A picture of the school Thobani attended

that as far as the subject content was concerned, the situation in the physical science classroom would have been better if the teacher had always been absent from class as even the practical work was non-existent. He says, 'If we did one practical during that year, it was a lot.'

Thobani believes that his teacher had neither any passion for the subject nor any interest in the learners. In consequence, the learners' self-esteem plummeted and they lacked confidence in responding to questions. He laments, 'We only skimmed the surface of what had to be learned for the exam, all on our own. When I chose the subject in Grade 10, I had high hopes of becoming an engineer.' However, this hope slowly faded as the result of having to cope with physical science as 'taught' by a teacher whom he describes as 'horrible' and 'knowing less' than the learners. In an attempt to seek help, Thobani and his fellow learners went to the principal's office to ask for a substitute, but without success. In response to a question whether the teacher was qualified to teach physical science, Thobani states, 'I don't know—we went to the office to find out if we can't get a substitute, but we never got a positive response. I can't even remember this teacher's name.'

In consequence of his unfavourable experience with physical science at school and poor matriculation results in the subject, Thobani could not gain entry to a university engineering programme. He blames his Grade-12 teacher for his misfortune which left him with no other choice but to opt for a teaching career instead. After entering the teaching profession, Thobani hoped to make a difference to the way physical science was being taught in schools and set himself the goal of achieving a 100 % pass rate. The following section presents a transcript of Thobani's responses in relation to the specific themes deduced from the interview transcript as a whole.

PORTRAITURE ANGLE: THOBANI'S VIEWS ON THE SHIFT FROM C2005 TO THE NCS

In this section Thobani describes how he experienced the shift from C2005 to the NCS. He explains what it was like in the early days of the implementation process and describes his struggle to overcome the many hindrances to his implementation of the NCS. Thobani explained,

> I entered the teaching profession as a physical science teacher in 1998. I started during a time when there was a lot of confusion. When I started teaching, it was the introduction of OBE. Many of us were confused but I was in a better position because I was fresh coming out of school [university].

When asked about the confusing period and why he thought he was in a better position, he replied,

> Most of the teachers, they did not know what to do, how to teach and the content—phew! They struggled [smiling]. I think they did not have better training but I learned a lot about the new curriculum at school [university]. I was better prepared than they because at least this new curriculum I was ready for it.

Thobani further describes how he struggled with his older colleagues who found it difficult to accept the new policy changes prescribed by the NCS and how their negative mindset regarding the NCS affected him. He said,

> You see, the people like my HOD [Head of Department], he's coming from the old way of teaching. The traditional, the old way, which was in the apartheid era. So we were always at loggerheads as to how much we must teach and how much mustn't we teach the learners.

When asked how he felt about the new curriculum changes (referring to the shift from C2005 to the NCS), he explained,

I was very happy because my learners they benefited. They were now better prepared for university. I did not do this new content [when he was a learner] that was now added to the curriculum but they did it, so that made me very happy. I use it to help them, my students. I always tell them it is a good thing this new shift to NCS.

At this point in the interview it was evident that Thobani favoured the new curriculum but that he was troubled by the opposition from his HOD and older colleagues. As he was searching through his memory and reflecting on his past experiences, he appeared to be reliving the accumulated effects of his experiences as a learner and the objections that he faced from his teaching colleagues many years later. The researcher (first author) noticed the seriousness and anger with which he spoke about how he felt at the time. The inner turmoil that he was experiencing was also evident from his facial expressions and gestures. While he was reflecting and speaking, his arms were tightly folded across his stomach as if in an attempt to contain himself and not to show too much emotion. His non-verbal gestures, the long pauses between responses and his choice of words appeared to be an attempt to find the appropriate words to describe his emotions. It represented a symbolic sense of his need to protect himself as well as an attempt on his part to express his agitation politely in the company of his older interlocutors. It can be assumed that he was well aware of the fact that his interlocutors did not support the curriculum change. Haney et al. (1996) note that when more experienced teachers are favourably disposed towards a curriculum change, it also inspires novice teachers to respond positively to the proposed policy changes in education.

THOBANI'S CLASSROOM EXPERIENCE AND INTERPRETATION OF THE NCS

Asked how he felt about the new NCS curriculum and whether he had implemented it in his classroom, Thobani had the following to say:

Phew! One has no choice but to apply the NCS because, you see, OBE goes along with lots of things. There are many things that one needs to *assess*—even the seating of the learners. You can't allow learners to be sitting alone or on their own. Now, teaching OBE, one has to teach with context in mind. I am there—I am comfortable with teaching with a context. I have always done that.

The image Thobani portrays about the NCS in the above quotation suggests that it requires new ideas and more effort for the assessment of tests and assignments, classroom management (seating arrangements), the application of knowledge (context) and preparation. His statements 'one has no choice' and 'there are many things one has to assess' subconsciously reflect the magnitude of the task of implementing the NCS. When he was asked how often he did practical work (see Table 4.1: LO 1: Practical investigation and problem-solving), he pointed out that time did not allow him to do as much practical work as he would have liked to do. He also complained about the lack of resources that hindered his ability to do practical work. He commented, 'I do at least one practical per term (every 4 months) because there is no equipment.' It should be borne in mind that the NCS requires teachers to use LO 1 of which ASs 1.1 and 1.3 should form the basis of the lessons they teach. When asked whether he understood the curriculum and what was demanded of him to be an effective implementer, he said,

> After 13 years of teaching, I must by now know and understand the curriculum. No, those concepts we have grasp them. They were a problem when the new syllabus was being introduced...We had to implement them but now after about 13 years of teaching I think I understand them.

When asked about how much time in his lessons he devoted to LO 3, specifically ASs 3.1 and 3.2, he pointed out that his focus was on teaching the content (LO 2). He said, 'I hardly have time to complete the content [LO 2: AS 2.1: Recalling and stating concepts], so I do that [LO 3] when I have time.' On the subject of assessment, he asserted that he assessed his learners regularly through activities such as workbook exercises, asking questions, tests, examinations and allowing the learners to work in groups (LO 2: ASs 2.1 and 2.2). He explained, 'All those tools I'm using them but, when it comes to assessment. I assess every day.' He reiterated that he did not experience any problems teaching the content. When asked if he understood the content, he replied,

> It takes a lot of my own time at home. I spent a lot of time on my own studying to understand the curriculum. Even the topics I made sure I understand. You know, what helped me would be the exemplars that were provided by the WCED [Western Cape Education Department]. I was never taught those topics at school, not even at *university*. I was never taught but most of the things that I am teaching currently I had to read them on my own to understand them.

The following citation describes what Thobani considered to be the most challenging part of implementing the NCS:

> My biggest challenge was, first of all, I did not know how to prepare my lessons with the different outcomes in mind. During that time, I only went to class not knowing while teaching whether I was meeting the demand of those critical and developmental outcomes but, after some time, *I learned* what was expected of me and did so.

When asked who had helped him to understand these outcomes, he stated that most of the work he had to learn on his own and added, 'I am a life-long learner and am slowly becoming a specialist.'

PORTRAITURE ANGLE: THOBANI'S VIEWS ON THE TRAINING OFFERED BY THE DEPARTMENT OF EDUCATION PRIOR TO THE IMPLEMENTATION OF THE NCS

The following quotation describes Thobani's view on the training he received:

> This training it was too short. Yo, yo, yo! I expected much more from these training sessions. It was a big joke and a real waste of my time. They could not fit into these sessions all the materials one needed to know...yo![4]

When asked whether or not the training was helpful, he had the following to say:

> I would say, if I can rate them [the workshops], they would be 20 % helpful. The other 80 % was more confusing. You know why I am saying so: it's because the WCED they took some of us [teachers] and made us curriculum advisors. Those curriculum advisors were the ones that were also confused. Those guys they were given the opportunity to come back to us. One could sense they were not confident—they did not know what they were saying in those workshops.

When asked how he felt about and *who* had arranged the workshops and *how* and *when* it had been done, he replied,

> I still remember, we'll stay after school when one is tired. We'll stay for two to four hours or on Saturdays two to four hours. That is the maximum time we spent on those workshops. Some of the workshops were also offered during the June holidays for a period of one week by the curriculum advisors.

Thobani felt that the training he had received raised more questions than it answered, which is why he constantly referred to the training sessions or workshops as confusing. He had hoped that the training offered by the WCED would allay all his fears, anxieties and insecurities and would adequately prepare him for the effective implementation of the NCS. Instead, he was left disappointed as he had to learn most of what he needed to know on his own. He pointed out in an earlier excerpt that the workshops were too short to fit in all the materials to be learnt, and in the above quotation, he highlights the fact that the training was offered during school holidays, weekends and after school when he needed to rest.

DISCUSSION

The 'Horrible Physical Science Teacher'

To understand Thobani's descriptive experiences more clearly, we, firstly, availed ourselves of the resources of Heideggerian phenomenology to write an interpretive narrative based on his responses. Heideggerian phenomenology allowed the researchers to give meaning to Thobani's experiences by providing an interpretive narrative based on the researcher's interaction with the interviewee. It allowed the researchers to connect the context within which the interviewee was teaching, the mood that existed during the interview, as well as the researchers' expert opinion on how they thought the interviewee experienced the phenomena. In this research project, it allowed the researchers to construct Thobani's phenomenological attitude towards physical science, which started at school when he was a learner. Secondly, we strove to present his views regarding the shift from C2005 to the NCS, Thirdly, the approach allowed us to discuss the perception of the influence and role his HOD and older colleagues played in the implementation, and, in conclusion, the poor training provided by the department of education.

Firstly, constructing an interpretive narrative from Thobani's biography was a complex task. The interview as a whole provided meaning and insight into specific events and how these events directed the course of his life. From this we could separate minor issues from major ones and deduce how the major events impacted on his being and becoming. Our personal experiences both as learners and as teachers of physical science (first and second author) and the major events that happened in Thobani's life allowed us entry into his consciousness to construct his biography.

Furthermore, our use of Heideggerian phenomenology in this section was intended to assist us in achieving a deeper insight into the objects of experience in his consciousness and did not in any way imply an intention on our part to critique his descriptions and other responses. Rather, it was our objective to reveal how the complex workings of his conscious as well as his subconscious mind influenced his understanding of physical science as a school subject.

What stands out in Thobani's biography was the negative influence that his teacher had on him as a learner and the environment in which he received his teaching. Throughout the interview he continually pointed out what a 'horrible physical science teacher' he had had. This experience had created the subconscious perception that physical science was a difficult subject. This is evident from his statement: '...We did not understand our teacher and went to the principal's office to ask for a substitute...' and from the fact that he lamented the poor examination results that prevented him from studying the subject of his dreams: engineering.

Many studies have shown that poor teaching leads to a poor understanding of science (e.g. see MacDonald and Rogan 1988; Ogunniyi 1996). Olitsky (2006, 209) argues that this problem is not confined to a lack of resources but is directly related to a teacher's inability to guide and nurture a learner to become a member of the scientific community. Olitsky (2006, 209) further argues that the learning of science is more than just a cognitive activity in that entails the development of a social identity associated with scientific practice and discourse that should start at school level. To acquire this kind of knowledge base in science, the learner needs to develop a sense of somehow belonging to the world of science, which could emerge from a strong relationship with his or her teacher.

In Thobani's case, the lack of both a role model and positive exposure to the teaching of physical science fostered a deep-seated resentment towards the teaching of the subject he loved and a psychologically ambivalent attitude towards science. The fact that Thobani's school teacher followed the doctrine of FP, as Clark and Linder (2006) argue, could have major implications for the way he (Thobani) views the subject. In his subconscious mind, science had become associated with an objective, distant and meaningless subject aggravated by his teacher's incompetence and narrow ways of looking at the world. Thobani's story begs the question to what extent his understanding of science would have been different if he had had a competent and passionate teacher with a sound understanding of science and what effect that would have had on his understanding of physical science. Basson and Kriek's (2012) study on physical science teaching found that at the core of effective science teaching is the need for teachers to possess specialised knowledge and skills which, Olitsky (2006) argues, should start at school level.

Thobani's Challenge of Dealing with His HOD and Older Colleagues

Mellville et al. (2011, 2276) assert that formidable challenges await teachers who are looking to contest the hegemony of traditional teaching strategies without sustained support to overcome such challenges. Bourdieu (1977) points out that social worlds, such as the science department in Thobani's school, are comprised of different social spaces or 'fields' within which individuals engage in contests. These contests occur between individuals whose dispositions or 'habitus'—the way they behave and feel—make them more likely or able to engage in the roles and responsibilities assigned to them in schools or other related fields. These social spaces are represented subconsciously to orient a person's awareness and actions. For this reason, individuals perceive the same opportunity differently because of their different dispositions. This could explain the responses of Thobani's colleagues, who may have developed or adopted a 'habitus' which defined the relationship between learners, the learning culture and its associated change differently from his. The upshot of this situation is usually 'a space of conflict' and competition: the older teachers dominate and the new ones struggle to have their voices heard.

Bantwini (2010) argues that at the heart of successful curriculum implementation is continuous professional development. At Thobani's school, professional development was non-existent and, instead of encouraging Thobani, who was fresh from university, his HOD and senior colleagues were opposed to his decision to implement the NCS and put many obstacles in his way. To aggravate matters, the workshops and training offered to him by the Department of Education as a form of professional development he found at best 'confusing' and 'a waste of time'. He pointed out that it was through self-study and sacrifice that he came to understand the curriculum and the new content associated with it. He mainly used the assessment tools provided by the department (such as specimen questions and answers, old question papers and examination guidelines) to plan and deliver the content to his learners. That he paid relatively little attention to LO 1 (ASs 1.1, 1.2, 1.3 and 1.4) and LO 3 (ASs 3.1, 3.2 and 3.4) and had to learn the curriculum on his own suggests that he moulded the curriculum to fit his context and understanding. Waugh and Punch (1987) contend that although teachers take ownership of curriculum change, the implemented curriculum is not always the enacted curriculum. According to Cuban (1998), this happens because teachers will adapt and modify the anticipated outcomes to suit their purpose. Therefore, the possibility exists that there might be a disjuncture between the teachers' conceptions and beliefs and those of the prescribed or intended curriculum. This raises the question of how Thobani perceived the NCS, based on his recollections as captured in the interview responses.

Heidegger's and Thobani's Epistemic Nature

Thobani's perceptions or consciousness of the NCS might best be explained using Heidegger's (1967) concepts of 'hammering' and 'the coping being'. According to Heidegger (1967), *dasein* (being in the situation) always involves a type of mood such as anxiety, anger or a feeling of being threatened, and so forth, as an emotional manifestation of the nature of the being. Heidegger argues that mood is always present in any situation and that when people enter a situation, they move in behind its mood. Heidegger uses the phrase *hammering* to explain what happens in the mind of a carpenter as he or she knocks the nails into a piece of wood while building a cupboard. Hammering comprises two processes, namely ready-to-handle and unready-to-handle situations (Heidegger 1967).

In the ready-to-handle situation (present at hand), the carpenter is not in a state of awareness as the process of using a hammer is transparent, self-evident and requires no thought. All that is important at that moment is the act of using the hammer to knock nails into wood or some other object. Heidegger describes the carpenter as being cognitively asleep or unaware of the situation or surroundings. This example of *hammering* depicts how not only craftspersons but also teachers go about their work unreflectively—that is, without questioning the status quo or giving any thought to the process. Like carpenters, teachers only work towards achieving their goal, which is to finish the project they are working on and to move on. The aforementioned reveals that teachers might have a particular understanding of the curriculum which they continue to follow/implement. Whether their understanding is authentic or unauthentic, their actions represent their psychological condition. Heidegger's main thesis is that one's psychological condition or state of mind is grounded primarily in "what has always been" (Heidegger 1967, 341). The latter becomes a mode of projectedness within which a person's mind becomes caged. However, the situation and the mood change into a state of heightened awareness on the part of the craftsperson when the use of the hammer becomes problematic or too difficult for the task at hand. Now the craftsperson is forced to make adjustments to the way the tool is being used by either modifying, repairing or replacing it. In this unready-to-handle situation, the coping part of the process represents the heightened state of cognitive awareness that forces the carpenter to observe the situation more closely and reflect on it in an attempt to ameliorate the situation. In the process, the carpenter's regular lifeworld is filled with uncertainty, confusion or disorder as he or she now has to think about what has been happening. Heidegger believes that we only become conscious when things go wrong. Furthermore, he argues that this new state of mind (heightened awareness) has its origin in "the temporality of concern" (Heidegger 1967, 400). Factually, this temporality of concern becomes necessary to approximate new goals which subsequently require a new way of 'seeing' or looking at the world (or some concept) which gives birth to new ideas or understanding. Similarly, teachers are forced out of their comfort zone when the prevailing policies, procedures or curricula become obsolete or when they are suddenly challenged or replaced.

In Thobani's case, he instinctively and intuitively responded to the challenge of finding a new phenomenological coping mechanism when the tools of his trade became ineffective due to the introduction of a new curriculum for physical science. Forced to adapt, Thobani now had to reflect deeply on how to replace the old, unreflective ways of doing things with a fundamentally new approach. This involved constant reflection and revision as he attempted to address the problematic areas of the curriculum. In the process, he managed to dismiss negative thoughts and ideas in order to accept the challenge of curriculum change while at the same time adopting a positive mindset and attitude. This mindset allowed him to see the NCS not as something forced upon him but as an opportunity for professional and inner growth. Accepting the challenge and cultivating a positive mindset—despite the many depressing obstacles put in his way—assisted him in acting out his convictions in such a way that he became tolerant, flexible and susceptible to change. In essence, what Thobani shows us is that there is no mystery to change—essentially, it is about accepting new ideas and making a cognitive leap to address new challenges.

CONCLUSION

This study presents a phenomenological recount of a physical science teacher's lived experiences while implementing the NCS. It provides both a descriptive narrative (using Husserlian phenomenology) and an interpretive narrative (using Heideggerian phenomenology) to report the findings. The study focuses on Thobani's experiences, the act of being per se and the process of being in the midst of the curriculum delivery process. We discover Thobani's fundamental relation to the curriculum, his peers and colleagues. The findings indicate that, from the outset, Thobani wanted to become an active implementer of the NCS despite struggling to understand the curriculum. His desire to implement the NCS is revealed by his responses to his peers. His account of being at loggerheads with his peers and his HOD points to his efforts to implement the curriculum. From a Heideggerian perspective, Thobani's existential experiences and the development of his phenomenological attitude might have emerged from various metaphysical and ethical experiences during childhood, namely his struggle as a learner of physical science.

The most striking finding about Thobani's childhood experiences is how an incompetent Grade-12 physical science teacher was responsible for his ending up in the teaching profession. Not only did this experience leave him with an inadequate understanding of physical science, but it made the process of implementing the NCS syllabus very difficult as he struggled to make sense of the content he was required to teach. Another significant finding is that the poor support and encouragement he received from his HOD and the departmental officials made it extremely difficult for him to implement a challenging new syllabus in the absence of the necessary institutional and collegial support. However, despite the undermining influence of the negative responses and repeated ridicule of some of his colleagues, Thobani still managed to hold onto his belief that the NCS curriculum prepares learners for a better future career in science, which motivated him to implement it. The latter is substantiated by the following excerpt: "They were now better prepared for university." Thobani's philosophy is not idealistic because, in his own consciousness, he sees himself as an active implementer of the NCS despite the challenges of poor support structures at school, the department's lack of good teacher training workshops in both content and curriculum studies and the absence of continuous professional development.

The data from the phenomenological interview generated a rich description of the formidable challenges teachers face with when confronted with a radical curriculum change. The data also provided a clear picture of the lifeworld of a black physical science teacher in an informal settlement. The insights gained from this study go beyond the factual theories and rhetoric and therefore assist curriculum planners and advisors to understand that successful curriculum implementation hinges on teachers. According to Clarke and Linder (2006), without considerable teacher support and development, curriculum initiatives will continue to fail. Therefore, this study provides compelling evidence of the crucial role that teachers play in determining what goes on in the science classroom and the long-term consequences it has for the learner.

This research highlights an important issue for the field of curriculum studies in South Africa, which raises a concern about the latest version of the NCS—the CAPS. This document is a highly prescriptive curriculum framework that dictates *when*, *what* and for *how long* topics should be taught and learned. Over the past few decades, curriculum discourses in South Africa have privileged the policy-maker's world (see Le Grange 2007) to such an extent that only one view of curriculum has been legitimated, namely curriculum-as-planned. Thobani's narrative, as reported in this study, highlights the importance of another view of curriculum: curriculum-as-lived—a view that recognises the lived or living experiences of teachers. Acknowledging curriculum-as-lived does not mean dismissing curriculum-as-planned but brings to the fore a tensioned space between the two views of curriculum that teachers (as illustrated in Thobani's narrative) negotiate daily—a space that has not been researched or theorised sufficiently in South Africa. We aver that greater recognition of this tensioned space could be pivotal in efforts to transform education in South Africa. Aoki (cited by Koopman et al. 2016, 20) lucidly describes this tensioned space as follows:

> It is in this space of between that our teachers, sensitive to both curriculum-as-planned and curriculum-as-lived, dwell, likely finding it a tensioned space of ambiguity, ambivalence, and uncertainty but simultaneously a vibrant site. It looks like a simple oppositional binary space, but it is not. It is as space of doubling, where we slip into the language of "both this and that, but neither this nor that" Our teachers slip into the language of "both plannable and unplannable, but neither strictly plannable nor strictly unplannable." Confusing? Yes, Confusingly complex? Yes. But nevertheless a site that beckons pedagogic struggle, for such as human site promises generative possibilities and hope. It is, indeed, a site of becoming, where newness can come into being.

NOTES

1. *Epochê* refers to the role of the researcher allowing the data to flow freely from the research participant while bracketing out his or her (researcher) own personal beliefs, feelings, perceptions and views so as not to contaminate the data.
2. The things themselves are the result of unveiling the subjective knowing or representations of the respondent as divulged in the course of the interview.
3. The dynamics of how a person's historical, social and political experiences are expressed in his consciousness.
4. 'Yo' is an expression of amazement in the black community in South Africa.

REFERENCES

Aldous, C. (2004). Science and mathematics teachers' perceptions of C2005 in Mpumalanga secondary schools. *African Journal of Research for Mathematics, Science and Technology Education, 8*(1), 65–76.

Basson, I., & Kriek, J. (2012). Are grades 10 - 12 physical science teachers equipped to teach physics. *Perspectives in Education, 30*(3), 110–127.

Bantwini, B. (2010). How teachers perceive the new curriculum reform: Lessons from a school district in the Eastern Cape Province, South Africa. *International Journal of Educational Development, 30*, 83–90.

Bennet, R. (2002). Unconscious consciousness in Husserl and Freud. *Phenomenology and the Cognitive Sciences, 1*, 327–351.

Bourdieu, P. (1977). *Outline of a theory of practice.* Cambridge: Cambridge University Press.

Brodie, K., Lelliot, A., & Davis, H. (2002). Forms and substance in learner-centred teaching: Teachers' take up from an in-service program in South Africa. *Teacher and Teacher Education, 18*(5), 541–559.

Brown, R. K. (1992). Max van Manen and pedagogical human science research. In W. F. Pinar & W. M. Reynalds (Eds.), *Understanding curriculum as phenomenological and deconstructed text* (pp. 44–63). New York: Teachers College Press.

Clarke, J., & Linder, C. (2006). *Changing teaching, changing times: Lessons from a South African township science classroom.* Rotterdam/Taipei: Sense Publishers.

Cuban, L. (1998). How schools change reforms: Redefining reform success and failure. *Teachers College Record, 99*(3), 453–477.

Department of Basic Education. (2002). *Revised National Curriculum Statement: Grades R–9 (Schools): Policy, Natural Sciences.* Pretoria.

Department of Basic Education. (2006a). *Physical Sciences National Curriculum Statement: Grades 10–12 (General).* Pretoria.

Department of Basic Education. (2006b). *National Curriculum Statement for Further Education and Training.* Discussion document. Pretoria.

Department of Basic Education. (2008). *National Curriculum Statement for Further Education and Training.* Discussion document. Pretoria.

Department of Education. (1997). *Curriculum 2005.* Retrieved from http://www.polity.org.za/govdocs/misc/curr2005html (Accessed November 13, 2013).

Department of Education. (2003). *National Curriculum Statement for Further Education and Training.* Discussion document. Pretoria.

Department of Education. (2008). *National Curriculum Statement for Further Education and Training for Physical Science.* Discussion document: Pretoria.

Domert, D., Airy, J., Linder, C., & Kung, R. L. (2007). An exploration of university physics students' epistemological mindsets towards the understanding of physics equations. *Nordidina, 1,* 15–29.

Gardamer, H. G. (1975). *Truth and method.* New York: Seabury.

Hammer, D. (1995). Epistemological considerations in teaching introductory physics. *American Journal of Physics, Physics Education Research Supplement, 68,* 52–59.

Haney, J. J., Czerniak, C. M., & Lumpe, A. T. (1996). Teacher beliefs and intentions regarding the implementation of science education reform standards. *Journal of Research in Science Teaching, 33,* 971–993.

Heidegger, M. (1967). *Being and time* (Macquarrie, J., & Robinson, E., Trans. from the German). London: SCM Press.

Heidegger, M. (2002). *The essence of truth* (Sadler, T., Trans. from the German). New York, NY: Continuum.

Husserl, E. (1970). *The crisis of the European sciences and transcendental phenomenology: An introduction to phenomenological philosophy* (Carr, D., Trans. from the German). Evanston, IL: North-Western University Press.

Husserl, E. (1975). *The Paris lectures* (P. Koesterbaum, Trans.). The Hague: Martinus Nijhoff.

Hycner, R. (1985). Some guidelines for the phenomenological analysis of interview data. *Human Studies, 8,* 279–303.

Jansen, J. (1999). A very noisy OBE: The implementation of OBE in Grade 1 classrooms. In J. Jansen & P. Christie (Eds.), *Changing curriculum: Studies on outcomes based education in South Africa* (pp. 1–15). Cape Town: Juta.

Jansen, J. D., & Christie, P. (Eds.) (1999). *Changing curriculum: Studies on outcomes-based education in South Africa.* Cape Town: Juta.

Koopman, O. (2013). *Teachers' experiences of Implementing the Further Education and Training Science Curriculum. An* unpublished doctoral thesis. Stellenbosch University, Stellenbosch.

Koopman, O., Le Grange, L., & De Mink, K. J. (2016). A narration of black physical science teachers' experiences of implementing a new curriculum. *Education as Change, 20*(1), 1–20.

Kriek, J., & Basson, I. (2008). Implementation of the new FET Physical Science curriculum: Teachers' perspectives. *African Journal of Science, Mathematics and Technology Education*, Special edition: 63–76.

Le Grange, L. (2007). (Re)thinking outcomes-based education: From arborescent to rhizomatic conceptions of outcomes (based-education). *Perspectives in Education, 25*(4), 79–85.

McDonald, M. A., & Rogan, J. M. (1988). Innovation in South African science education: Science teaching observed. *Science Education, 72*(2), 225–236.

Mellville, W., Hardy, I., & Bartley, A. (2011). Bourdieu, department chairs and the reform of science education. *International Journal of Science Education, 33*(16), 2275–2293.

Miles, M. B., & Huberman, A. M. (1984). *Qualitative data analysis: A sourcebook of new methods*. Newbury Park, CA: Sage.

Nakedi, M., Taylor, D., Mundalamo, F., Rollnick, M., & Mokeletche, M. (2012). The story of a physical science curriculum: Transformation or transmutation. *African Journal of Mathematics Science and Technology Education, 6*(3), 273–288.

Ogunniyi, M. B. (1996). Science, technology and mathematics: The problem of developing critical human capital in Africa. *International Journal of Science Education, 18*(3), 267–284.

Olitsky, S. (2006). Facilitating identity formation, group membership, and learning in science classrooms. *Science Education, 10*, 201–223.

Rogan, J. M. (2004). Out of the frying pan…? Case studies of the implementation of Curriculum 2005 in some science classrooms. *African Journal of Science, Mathematics and Technology Education, 8*(2), 165–179.

Rogan, M. R., & Grayson, D. J. (2003). Towards a theory of curriculum implementation with particular reference to science education in developing countries. *International Journal of Science Education, 25*(10), 1171–1204.

Van Manen, M. (1984). Practising phenomenological writing. *Phenomenology and Pedagogy, 2*(1), 36–69.

Waugh, R. F., & Punch, K. F. (1987). Teacher receptivity to system-wide change in the implementation phase. *Review of Educational Research, 57*(3), 237–257.

CHAPTER 5

Do Teachers also See What Chemists See When They Teach Chemistry?

INTRODUCTION

The study on which this research is based stemmed from a collaborative project between academics from three South African universities and the Department of Basic Education (DBE) in the Limpopo province. Before the commencement of the project, the DBE had expressed concern about the inadequate content knowledge (CK) and pedagogical content knowledge (PCK) of science teachers instructing Grades 9–12 in the province. Their concern was based on the poor test scores of learners in systemic evaluations and examinations over the last three years. Based on this premise, one of the aims of the project entitled '(Re)-thinking Mathematics and Science Through the Lens of Phenomenology' is to assist teachers in improving their CK and PCK. To this purpose, 15 'lead' teachers and 2 science education specialists were selected by the department to participate in the project. Lead teachers are chosen in cluster meetings and are normally more experienced than others. They are considered competent in their subject field and have a record of excellent results. After they had been empowered with CK and PCK, the lead teachers were required to share their experiences and expertise with others and mentor novice teachers in their districts. Some of the lead teachers were heads of department and others were deputy principals in their schools. The teachers represented 15 different districts in Tshivenda. The facilitators presenting the workshops were a consortium of academics from three different

© The Author(s) 2017
O. Koopman, *Science Education and Curriculum in South Africa*,
DOI 10.1007/978-3-319-40766-1_5

universities, specialising in mathematics, chemistry, physics, zoology and botany, respectively.

The South African government makes massive monetary investments annually to improve the quality of school science. Consequently, teachers are placed under pressure to produce good results in the sciences. The mounting pressure on teachers is exacerbated by increased media coverage and public debates on the poor quality of mathematics and science. At the core of such pressure is the realisation that a nation's standard of achievement and competitiveness depend on a highly educated and well-trained scientific community. For this reason, Lingard, Hayes, Mills and Christie (2003) draw attention to the cardinal importance of teachers, whom they metaphorically describe as the midwives of the new knowledge economy. They argue that without the teachers' commitment, the future will be 'malformed and stillborn' (ibid, vi). It follows that it is by no means coincidental that government should allocate the lion's share of the annual budget to education.

The last two decades have witnessed a growing concern about the poor subject knowledge and PCK of science teachers (Foundation for Research and Development Report 1993; Taylor and Vinjevold 1999; Naidoo and Lewin 1998; Koopman 2013). These concerns are based on the assumption that a distorted image of science by teachers can impede the efficient practice of science education. Taylor and Vinjevold's (1999) research into the CK of mathematics and science teachers in South Africa revealed that teachers struggle to deliver the content in a meaningful way. Basson and Kriek (2012) found similar evidence and raised major concerns about the teaching of science in township and rural schools. A survey conducted among 68 science teachers in such schools revealed that more than 80 % found the content intimidating and above their teaching ability. The researchers concluded that 88 % of the teachers in those areas were unqualified to teach science. Studies conducted by Naidoo and Lewin (1998), Ogunniyi (1988), Rogan and Grayson (2003) and Koopman (2013) found that because of the poor CK of science teachers and the fact that some teachers are trapped in traditional pedagogies, learners perceive the subject as difficult and oppressive. Internationally, researchers such as Jegede (1999), Hurd (2002), Osborne, Simon and Collins (2010), Price and McNeill (2013) share similar sentiments and echo the growing concern over the instrumental nature of science teaching and its associated effects on the learning of the subject. Although research into the epistemological conceptions of teachers' CK does occur, there is a dearth of empirical studies in South Africa.

The existence of such a significant research gap prompted me to embark on this project to research the question: How do science teachers intellectually engage with all three levels of representation of chemistry when they teach? Specifically, the research study aimed to determine and report on the science teachers' understanding of selected chemistry topics and how the teachers integrate the macro, submicro and symbolic levels when they deliver the content to their learners. The findings of this study are important in shedding light on curriculum development and the training of in-service teachers.

THREE LEVELS OF REPRESENTATION

Scholars from different parts of the world adopt various naming systems for the three levels of representation for objects in chemistry. For example, Andersson (1986) refers to it as the 'macroscopic' and 'atomic world'; Bodner (1992) uses the terms 'macroscopic', 'molecular' and 'symbolic' chemistry, whereas Johnstone (1993) calls it 'macro', 'submicro' and 'representational' chemistry. To avoid ambiguity, the study used the terms *macroscopic, submicroscopic* and *symbolic*, at an individual level and in a triplet relationship, to encompass all three levels (see Fig. 5.1).

According to Treagust, Chittleborough and Mamiala (2003), who conducted a similar study in Australia, the macroscopic level of representation points to the observable chemical phenomena that individuals experience through the use of their senses. It involves a wide range of observation skills

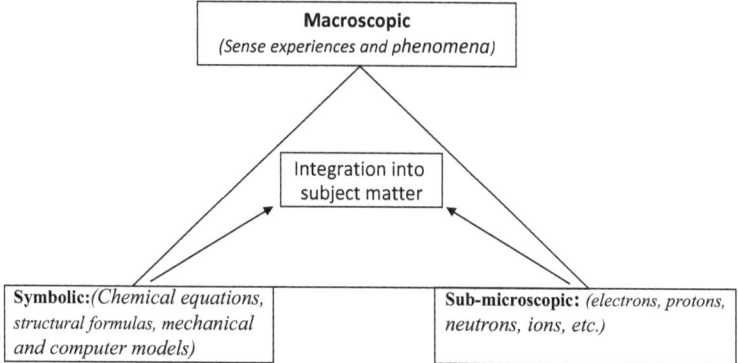

Fig. 5.1   Levels of representation of chemistry
Source: Adapted from Treagust, Chittleboroughand Mamiala (2003)

such as colour changes, alterations in shape when new products are formed and reactants disappearing. Locke (2009) argues that when individuals experience phenomena through their senses (sight, smell, touch, sound and taste), the sensual encounter penetrates deep into their minds, creating several distinct perceptions based on the peculiar properties of sensual contact. The brain retains these observed sensory images and leaves an impression which is stored in our long-term memory (see Locke 2009). Chemists routinely communicate macroscopic events using symbolic levels that include "pictorial, algebraic, physical and computational forms such as chemical equations, graphs, reactions mechanisms, analogies and model kits" (Treagust et al. 2003, 1354). Gilbert and Treagust (2009) describe microscopic-level entities as involving particles that cannot be seen with the naked eye and require chemists to extend the capacity of their senses by using optical microscopes. To explain these observations (of subatomic particles), chemists often build models of entities such as atoms, molecules and free radicals. The material world at its foundational level is made up of submicroscopic particles and is synonymous with the DNA of objects. This means that the answer to the internal and external properties of objects—such as shapes, colours, brittleness, tensile strength and toughness—is to be found at the submicroscopic level. Understanding the microscopic world of objects requires an understanding of the electrical properties of atoms, bonding angles, bonding energies, bond lengths, electron densities and the movements of orbital and interstitial objects. Harrison and Treagust (2002) explain that, at submicroscopic level, a range of misconceptions exists among students and teachers due to the particulate nature of matter, the inability of human beings to engage with it physically and their need to rely on imaginary images.

It follows that a good understanding of chemistry hinges on how well a teacher can establish the interrelationship between these three levels of representation because the symbolic and submicroscopic levels contain the theory that explains the macroscopic representation of objects. As Bucat and Mocerino (2009, 12) explain, "Seeing as chemist is a fact supported, theory laden exercise of a lively imagination." In other words, good chemistry teachers give their learners insight into the deeper meaning behind facts and allow them to see what chemists see when they observe a phenomenon. The opposite is also true as science teachers with inadequate CK of the triplet levels of representation can create serious obstacles to their learners' ability to understand chemistry. Therefore, Treagust, Chittleborough and Mamiala (2003) assert that expert chemistry teachers (1) deliver the content in a meaningful way that connects the three levels of representation at a level appropriate for the learners, (2) use relevant artefacts, (3) embrace the learners' prior knowledge of phenomena, (4) present the content without oversimplifying it and (5) challenge the learners. Kozma and Russell (1997) aver that novices in turn use only one form of representation, fail to convert to other levels, and consequently focus only on the macroscopic descriptions. Van Berkel et al. (2009) assert that most novice teachers are textbook-bound and reproduce superficial chemical explanations. This is because textbook writers generally represent expert chemistry knowledge superficially and therefore create misconceptions in explaining naturally occurring processes and events. Cheng and Gilbert (2009) report that instead of teachers invoking the skills to connect with all three levels of representation in the science classroom, learners have to rely on diagrams, visual aids and pictures in textbooks to make the representational connections with chemical processes such as the movement of electrons during electrolysis, electrochemical cells and in the Haber–Bosch process.

A Brief Description of the Teaching of Science in South Africa

Several South African studies show that science teachers frequently encourage rote learning (Muwanga-Zake (2008); Rogan and Grayson 2003; Rollnick et al. (2004); Koopman 2013). In such a paradigm, learners rely heavily on memorisation to pass examinations. According to Chisholm and Wildeman (2013, 90), this instrumental approach to teaching science comes as no surprise since high-stake examinations already existed as early as 1915. The authors further point out that after the transition to democracy in 1994, South Africa adopted a 'post-bureaucratic model' of accountability (Chisholm and Wildeman 2013, 90), in which the quality of teaching was measured by learner performance as a strategic plan to monitor teachers. The emphasis placed on learner performance as a measure of teacher effectiveness encourages teachers to neglect the foundational knowledge learners require to master any subject (Chisholm and Wildeman 2013). This, they argue, undermines the purpose of education. Such a system leaves learners underprepared, with no confidence or competence in science. This target-setting agenda encourages teachers to 'teach to the test'. In so doing, teachers confuse the learners by providing obscure and limited knowledge of the respective disciplines. This begs the question: What types of explanations do South African teachers provide in the chemistry classroom? To answer this question, the study drew on the work of Treagust et al. (2003).

SOUTH AFRICAN TEACHERS' DIFFERING VERBAL EXPLANATIONS IN CHEMISTRY

Treagust et al. (2003) collapsed Mamiala and Treagust's (2001) framework of 20 different types of possible teacher explanations in chemistry into the 5 most popular explanations. These findings were derived from data collected in South African classrooms. These findings are as follows: (1) *analogical,* in that teachers use personal real-life experiences to explain unfamiliar concepts and phenomena; (2) *anthropomorphic,* as they reduce complex scientific concepts to recognisable human qualities; (3) *relational,* because teachers draw on their own personal engagement with objects or events to explain phenomena; (4) *problem-based,* because concepts are explained by drawing on hypothetical problems as a basis to connect with the content, which is common in calculations and (5) *model-based,* as scientific models are used to explain something. The study put these explanations under the microscope to describe how the teachers in the study connected and engaged with the content of chemistry in the science classroom.

The microscopic level is often considered a complex terrain for teachers because it requires the use of accurate and meticulous descriptive language. This level of representation, Van Berkel et al. (2009) argue, is best left to the learner's imagination, instead of teachers attempting to explain and describe this level, which could lead to possible misconceptions. When teachers leave the microscopic level of explanation to the learner's imagination, teachers develop and instil open-mindedness and creativity in their learners. This holds true, they argue, because it indirectly encourages learners to become co-inquirers in the process, thereby allowing them space for personal engagement with the submicroscopic level. To measure how teachers engage with content, the framework developed by Treagust et al. (2003) will be complemented with activity theory.

ACTIVITY THEORY

Activity theory has developed over three generations of research (Engeström 2001). The third generation of ideas and developments focuses on the 'third space', that is, the classroom environment in which the world of the teacher collides with the world of the learner. Consequently, this space concentrates on 'what is learned' and 'how it is learned', which transcends both worlds. In the 'third space' (ibid, 137), the research approach concentrates on the discourse of the two interacting activity systems (teacher and learner). It traces the action of the object (learner or teacher) from an unreflected 'raw object' to a meaningful object constructed by the activity system.

Due to the fact that this study was conducted in a conference venue, the availability of resources might have affected teacher's decision-making processes. Activity theory was applied in a narrow sense as it took into account only the teaching process, namely the teachers, the learners, the division of labour between teachers, the discipline of chemistry and the rules that guide and drive the discipline. The context in which learning takes place is central to activity theory. Essentially, the study was more interested in how the teachers engaged with the content and how their peers (co-practitioners) jointly acted as members of the teaching community to achieve the outcome of the lesson which was the bringing together of all levels of representation in selected chemistry lessons. In other words, the study was more concerned with whether the teachers understood the discipline of chemistry, the level of engagement with the content and how the learners (peers) responded to the content.

METHODOLOGY

Ethical Issues

This qualitative study was situated within an interpretive framework. When we applied for ethical clearance for this project, the Department of Education requested a meeting with the principal investigators, researchers and facilitators. During this meeting, the department officials raised their concerns about the poor CK of teachers and insisted that one of the objectives of the project should be to improve the subject CK and PCK of the selected teachers. In addition, the department made the following recommendations:

1. The researchers must make the participating teachers aware of their rights.
2. Teachers should be informed about the project in writing and be given a summary of the goals, aims and objectives before commencement of the workshops.
3. Notes, questionnaires, diagnostic tests, achievement tests and interview schedules should be discussed, clarified and scrutinised for possible violation of teacher's rights.

Suggestions were made as to where and when the workshops should take place. It was decided that the workshops should take place during the first week of the June holidays and that teachers should be taken outside the district to a private secluded venue to avoid any distractions or disturbances related to family obligations.

The researchers agreed with the above suggestions and addressed all the concerns raised. For example, a review of the data-collection instruments was resubmitted to the department after which ethical approval was granted and the list of teachers finalised.

The Research Participants

The selected participant teachers were all lead teachers, mother-tongue speakers of Tshivenda, and representative of 15 district offices in Limpopo province. Four teachers were females and eleven were male. The selection criteria were based on their years of experience, the results of the learners in their subject over the last three years, and on their qualifications, age and seniority in their schools. Three of the fifteen teachers were deputy principals, two were heads of departments, one was a curriculum advisor and the remaining nine teachers were all at post-level one, with many years of experience. Only one of the teachers had limited experience of 2 years, whereas all the others had between 12 and 25 years of experience.

Data Collection

Although this study only reported on the lesson presentations of two teachers, a total of five lessons were presented. The teachers were divided into five groups of three teachers per group. Each group had to plan and present a lesson of their choice according to the Grade-10 syllabus. The brief given to the teachers was as follows:

1. One aspect of the syllabus should be taken, planned and presented as a 30-minute lesson.
2. Each lesson has to include all three levels of representation in chemistry, which must be integrated into the content.
3. The lesson should address the historical development of scientific knowledge over the centuries.
4. The content must be relevant and captivating to the learners.
5. The prior knowledge of the learners (audience) must be tested.
6. The content must be challenging and not oversimplified.

The teachers were given three hours to exchange ideas and to construct their lessons. These group discussions between the teachers were facilitated by the researcher. They were allowed to use as many sources as they can such as textbooks, laptops and/or cell phones to access the internet to make the lessons as interesting as possible. After the teachers indicated that they had finalised their lessons, the lesson was presented, in which each individual had to make a contribution which was observed and video-recorded. Field notes were also made. After each presentation, the lesson was dissected to determine whether or not the presenter had integrated the three levels of representation in the content. Their responses were probed where necessary to ensure that there were no misconceptions or misunderstandings. The lesson observations, video recordings and lesson discussions revealed that the lessons presented focused mainly on macroscopic and, to a small extent, on the symbolic levels. No switch between the three levels of representation had been made, and the teachers had ignored the submicroscopic level.

FINDINGS

The data presented below focused on the following aspects:

1. the content to be learned;
2. the historical development of scientific knowledge over the years;
3. the manner in which the teacher used the macroscopic level of representation to create a context for the content;
4. whether or not the teacher included the symbolic and submicroscopic levels of description of the content;
5. the manner in which the teacher switched between the different levels of representation to explain a concept.

LESSON 1: THE PERIODIC TABLE

The lesson started with the teacher explaining the LOs or specific aims for the lesson. The following excerpts highlight the main points raised in the lesson:

> Teacher: Today we are going to discuss the periodic table [teacher pointing to the periodic table on the big screen in front of the class], and at the end of the lesson, I hope that all of you will have understood the meaning of the periodic table in the chemistry classroom. We will look at the

different groups and periods on the periodic table. We will consider why the different elements are found where they are on the periodic table and what they have in common. Do you all understand?

Class: *Yes, sir.*

Teacher: *As far as the periodic table is concerned, I often look at it as a bible. When you go to church, you carry a bible with you, so the preacher uses the bible to teach you about God. I want you to know that just as the preacher knows the bible, chemistry uses the periodic table to explain everything. The most important periodic laws are the groups and the periods. Groups are the vertical rows of elements, whereas the horizontal rows are referred to as the periods. As indicated here [teacher pointing to the different groups on the periodic table], we have Group 1, 11, up until Group 8. Sometimes these groups will be shown by means of numbers or Roman figures. Roman figures 1, 2 ... 7 and 8 [I, II, VII and VIII]. These Roman figures will be of use when we consider the valence electron. It will be easier for us to follow and find the different groups by looking at the Roman figures. Group number 1, Roman figure 1[I], are called alkali-metals ... Group 7 [VII] are called the halogens. The last one, Group number 8 [VIII]), are called inert gases or noble gases. They are also identified as the kings on the periodic table. They don't mix with the other elements if they don't have to. Therefore, all the other elements on the periodic table aspire to be like them. We also have between Groups 2 and 3 the transition elements.*

These elements have been arranged in order of their atomic number. The atomic number is the number of protons found in the elements. If we choose Hydrogen, with the symbol (H), it is number one there [pointing to the screen]. It means it has how many electrons?

Class: *One.*

Teacher: *That is correct, and that one electron is found in the first energy level. In each and every element we have levels, called energy levels or shells, in which the electrons are indicated. As the atomic number will be increasing, the number of shells will be increasing. We also have the metals and non-metals. You see this zigzag line here (highlighted in red), to the left of this line we find all the metals and to the right we find the non-metals. There are different elements to the right of the line or the non-metal side that occurs naturally as diatomic elements. In an equation, we write it as Cl_2, H_2 ... The question is how are we going to determine these diatomic elements? We must have a key and we do have one—it is called CONFIB. C stands for chlorine, O for oxygen ... and B for bromine...*

LESSON 1: DISCUSSION

In this lesson the teachers used a variety of resources. They used the data projector to display the periodic table on the big screen and a flip chart and a felt-tip pen to illustrate and explain important concepts and relationships between terms. The periodic table was clearly visible on the big screen throughout the lesson, which to some extent contributed to meaningful learning as the learners could locate and link the various groups and periods on the periodic table. For example, they could see how the elements are arranged from left to right with increasing atomic numbers in periods and in groups from top to bottom. The teachers used the flip chart to explain important concepts and terms that needed clarification, such as the differences between groups, and so forth.

They (teachers) did not invite discussion among the learners, nor did they create opportunities for the learners to demonstrate their own understanding or misunderstanding of the main concepts and definitions. They (teacher) were disconnected from the learners as they remained in front of the classroom for the duration of the lesson. This did not allow teacher–learner interactions to occur and create an interactive classroom environment that is important for effective science teaching and learning (Hurd 2002; Osborne et al. 2010). The focus of the lesson was mainly on symbols and rules that guide the arrangement of elements on the periodic table. No in-depth understanding of the content was displayed, and learners were not effectively guided to take responsibility for their own learning such as following up on the content that was discussed in the lesson.

The teachers used an array of anthropomorphic explanations when they compared the periodic table to the bible, the description of the 'zigzag' line for separating metals from non-metals and when they referred to the Group 8 elements as 'kings'. They reportedly stated, '*They [teacher pointing to Group 8 elements] don't mix with the other elements.' Furthermore, one of the teachers in the group developed a long acronym or rhyme as a key to unlock the location of the diatomic elements on the periodic table.* These comments are consistent with the framework on teacher explanations in chemistry developed by Treagust et al. (2003) and Mamiala and Treagust (2001). These researchers argue that teachers often resort to anthropomorphic explanations when they use human characteristics to describe non-human qualities. Tuckey and Selvanatram (1993) argue that because learners cannot visualise such explanations due to a lack of personal engagement, they could easily misinterpret the explanations for lack of scientific rigour and accuracy. This becomes more complicated when teachers use explanations that learners cannot relate to in their everyday experiences with the concept. The findings are consistent with Van Berkel, Pilot and Bulte's (2009) findings, who assert that most teachers are too textbook-bound that results in superficial explanations of chemistry. They averse that this hold true because textbook writers generally represent expert chemistry knowledge superficially and therefore create misconceptions in explaining naturally occurring processes and events.

The teachers focused mainly on the symbolic level of representation. In summary, the lesson underscored the different chemical symbols, the position of the elements on the periodic table (the respective groups), the names of the groups and group numbers and the horizontal periods. Although the lesson included the submicroscopic aspects, where the link was made between the proton number and the number of protons in the nucleus and the number of electrons, it was disconnected from the wider macroscopic world of real-life phenomena. Indeed, such phenomena (macroscopic level) can only be understood when a learner is introduced to corpuscular building blocks of chemistry such as the atom, ions and molecules, which are all embedded in the content derived from the periodic table. For example, a descriptive in-depth understanding of the periodic table provides insight into aspects related to the electrical neutrality, ionisation energy, the radius of the atom, and so forth, which is needed to explain the behaviour of objects at microscopic level. In the post-lesson discussion, when the teachers were asked why they had ignored the macroscopic level and its relation to real-world experiences, they said, *'Well, we will have to read up more on that because it's not easy to relate elements to its [their] natural occurrences.'* When asked why they refer to the periodic as a bible, one teacher commented, *'To us Christians nothing is more important than the bible, so I suppose nothing is as important as the periodic table when studying chemistry.'*

The development of the periodic table has a long and interesting history, which was not discussed. For example, approximately 2400 years ago only seven elements were known. Between 1600 and 1776 more elements were added until a breakthrough was made by Dimitri Mendeleyev. Although the teachers mentioned Mendeleyev's contribution in passing, they could not explain in detail how Mendeleyev had arrived at his conclusions about the periodic table—that is, how Mendeleyev's obsession with cards assisted him in identifying the missing elements. This discovery gave rise to the modern periodic table. This information is important as learners need to become familiar with the conceptual models of the periodic table that were developed throughout history so that they can discover why one historical model replaced another. This requires the teacher to convey knowledge and carefully explain how the knowledge came into existence. This information often requires an in-depth understanding of the symbolic and submicroscopic levels.

Lesson 2: Acids and Bases

Teacher: *I have just come from the market where I saw lots of fruit and I was wondering how many types of fruit I saw there were acids and bases. I could only afford to buy some oranges, so I want us to test whether oranges are acidic or basic. So, in today's lesson we are going to look at acids and bases. But before we do that, can anyone tell me what is an acid and what is a base?*

Class: *An acid tastes sour, Sir, and it has corrosive properties, whereas a base taste bitter and is not corrosive. For example, a car battery is acidic and it can damage your clothes and skin if it falls on it, whereas the soap that we wash with is a base. It does not damage your skin when you wash with it.*

Teacher: *That is correct. What they forget to tell us is that an acid has a pH of below 7. That is from 1 to 7 is an acid. A base has a pH of above 7. So it falls in between 7 and 14. Therefore 7 is now included and should be neutral. We must not forget that some substances are strong acids, for example, battery acid, is a strong acid because it has a pH of 3. That is why it burns the skin and clothes. But the vinegar at home, which you use for your fish and chips, that one is a weak acid. It has a pH of 6. So it is not a strong acid but a weak acid. Therefore, you can even drink it and nothing serious will happen to you. But if you drink battery acid, you will die. [Teacher continues to tell a story of battery acid...]. To test acids and bases we use litmus paper. Does anyone know what litmus paper is?*

Class: *You get different colour litmus paper. It is an indicator and changes colour when placed in an acid solution unlike in a basic solution.*

Teacher: *Okay, you guys are too clever for me [teacher smiling]. Now, please split up into groups of 4 learners per group. I want each group to come to the front and to collect an orange and litmus paper. I want you to cut the orange in half and squeeze the juice into a glass with a little water in it. What I want you to do is to determine whether the substance is an acid or a base.*

Class: *Groups following instructions. Lesson continues ...*

LESSON 2: DISCUSSION

In this lesson the teachers used a problem-based approach to differentiate between acids and bases. Such an approach involves explaining a concept by drawing on a hypothetical problem as a basis to convey the content verbally. Evident in such explanations is the use of calculations, numbers and figures to explain phenomena. In this lesson the teachers used the example of 'battery acid' and 'vinegar' to explain what an acid is. They also assigned pH values to differentiate between pH strengths. They did not draw on theory to explain these differences, nor did they give any causal scientific explanations for their statements. Instead, their definitions of acids and bases were based on pH values. The experiment in which learners were required to measure the pH of oranges was insignificant if it was not contextualised or socially meaningful. A context creates interest among learners and serves as a basis to introduce the learner to more complex theoretical explanations for chemical behaviour.

If these explanations are not made with care, teachers might create confusion or naïve conceptions in chemistry. One essential component missing from this lesson was the epistemological duty of the teacher to guide the learners to distinguish between the different chemical models of acids and bases by introducing them to their symbolic and submicroscopic properties. In this lesson on acid–base properties, the teacher focused mainly on the macroscopic levels of representation. The gradual development of our knowledge about acid–base reactions started as early as in the ninth century. The teachers in this study ignored the long history of knowledge about acids and bases. For example, as long ago as in the ninth century, vinegar (in *Latin*: acetum) and base (from *Arabic*: which means *ashes*) were characterised and described as sour and bitter. During that period, Arrhenius' electrolytic dissociation of acid and bases was unknown. In other words, in this lesson, the teacher gave his learners a ninth-century definition of an acid and a base. Boyle introduced us to the use of indicators in 1661already when he observed how an acid turned a violet vegetable extract red and a base blue. Again, in this regard, the teacher's conceptual model of explanations was outdated. When asked in a post-lesson interview why the teachers defined it in this way, they responded, *'Well, this is how the textbook describes it. Also, learners come to me from lower grades with this knowledge about acids and bases.'* The teachers' response is consistent with the view of Berkel et al. (2009) that textbooks are flawed with misconceptions and inaccurate descriptions. Consequently, teachers must question textbook definitions and descriptions in order to challenge the misconceptions learners have about school science.

In order for learners to understand the theory behind the macroscopic observable behaviour of acids and bases, such as their corrosive and sour taste properties, they need to understand the symbolic and submicroscopic aspects of the content. Arrhenius characterised these properties as long ago as in 1884 when he described an acid as a substance which, when dissolved in water, increases the hydrogen ion (H^+) concentration of the solution, whereas a base, when dissolved in water, increases the hydroxide ion $(OH-)$ concentration. His theory solved some of the most important problems in science: it explained the acidic and basic properties of aqueous salts. In 1923, Lowry-Brønsted provided a new set of data and consequently proposed a new theory that explained the concepts of acids and bases in which an acid is defined as having elemental properties to donate protons and a base as a proton acceptor. Today, we know how to diagnose and treat diseases such as arthritis and abdominal bloating related to acids and bases.

CONCLUSION

The study discussed in this chapter investigated how science teachers in the Limpopo province of South Africa intellectually engaged with the content of chemistry at the macroscopic, submicroscopic and symbolic levels. The theories needed to understand and explain macroscopic behaviour can be found at the submicroscopic and symbolic levels of representation. The findings of Lesson 1 show how the teacher relied on anthropomorphic explanations to deliver the content. These types of explanations have the potential to create confusion and misconceptions about scientific concepts if learners cannot relate them to real-life examples to explain phenomena. Furthermore, the lesson focused mainly on the symbolic level of representation and to a lesser extent on the submicroscopic level. When the symbolic and submicroscopic levels of representation are omitted from the teaching and learning of chemistry, science is reduced to conceptual knowledge, thus rendering it devoid of interest. Such a narrow view of science could create serious obstacles for learners trying to understand their lifeworld. In Lesson 2, the teacher relied on problem-based explanations even though such explanations are often considered confusing and lacking in rigour and scientificity. Furthermore, the teacher only used the macroscopic level of representation and ignored the submicroscopic and symbolic levels. In the teaching of a topic such as acids and bases, theory is important because it embodies the deeper layers of meaning that explain how and why a substance behaves in a specific way.

In conclusion, the findings of the study clearly show that the teachers failed to engage with the content at all three levels. This raises serious questions about the training of preservice and in-service chemistry teachers, besides having serious implications for curriculum development in South Africa. The challenge the chemistry teachers face in South Africa is to evolve suitable didactic practices to preserve its unity at all three levels of representation. The reason is that these levels of representation give insight into the gradual development of knowledge over the centuries, demonstrate that scientific knowledge is not stationary and provide insight into how scientific theories and laws are formulated.

REFERENCES

Andersson, B. (1986). Pupils' explanations of some aspects of chemical reactions. *Science Education, 70*, 549–563.

Basson, I., & Kriek, J. (2012). Are grades 10 - 12 physical science teachers ready to teach physics? *Perspectives in Education, 30*(3), 110–127.

Bodner, G. M. (1992). Refocusing the general chemistry curriculum. *Journal of Chemical Education, 69*, 186–190.

Bucat, B., & Mocerino, M. (2009). Learning at the sub-micro level: Structural representations. In J. Gilbert & D. Treagust (Eds.), *Multiple representations in chemical education: Models and modeling in science education* (pp. 11–29). Springer.

Cheng, M., & Gilbert, J. (2009). Towards a better utilization of diagrams research into the use of representative levels in chemical education. In J. Gilbert & D. Treagust (Eds.), *Multiple representations in chemical education: Models and modeling in science education* (pp. 55–73). Springer.

Chisholm, L., & Wildeman, R. (2013). The politics of testing in South Africa. *Journal of Curriculum Studies 45*(1), 89–100.

Engeström, Y. (2001). Expansive learning at work: Toward an activity theory reconceptualization. *Journal of Education and Work, 14*, 143–156.

Foundation for Research and Development. (1993). South African science and technology indicators: Foundation for research and development. Pretoria.

Gilbert, J., & Treagust, D. (2009). Introduction: Macro, sub-micro and symbolic representations and the relationship between them: Key models in chemical education. In J. Gilbert & D. Treagust (Eds.), *Multiple representations in chemical education: Models and modeling in science education* (pp. 11–19). Springer.

Harrison, A. G., & Treagust, D. F. (2002). Secondary students' mental models of atoms and molecules: Implications for teaching chemistry. *Science Education, 80*(5), 509–534.

Hurd, P. D. (2002). Modernizing science education. *Journal of Research in Science Teaching, 39*(1), 3–9.

Jegede, O. (1999). Science education in non-western cultures: Towards a theory of collateral learning. In L. Semali & J. Kincheloe (Eds.), *What is indigenous knowledge? Voices from the academy* (pp. 119–142). New York: Falmer Press.

Johnstone, A. H. (1993). The development of chemistry teaching: A changing response to a changing demand. *Journal of Chemical Education, 70*(9), 701–705.

Koopman, O. (2013). Teachers' experiences at implementing the Further Education and Training science curriculum. An unpublished doctoral. Stellenbosch University. Stellenbosch.

Kozma, R., & Russel, J. (1997). Multimedia and understanding: expert and novice responses to different representations of chemical phenomena. *Journal of Research in Science Teaching, 34*, 949–968.

Lingard, B., Hayes, D., Mills, M., & Christie, L. (2003). *Leading learning.* Maidenhead Philadelphia: Open University Press.

Locke, J. (2009). *Of the abuse of words.* London: Penguin Books.

Mamiala, T. L., & Treagust, D. F. (2001). *Teachers' use of explanations in high school chemistry. Paper presented at the annual meeting at the national associations for Research in Science Teaching.* MO: St Louis.

Muwanga-Zake, J. W. (2008). Is science education in a crisis: Some of the problems in South Africa. Science in Africa, Africa's first online magazine, www.scienceinafrica.co.za/scicrisis.htm.

Naidoo, P., & Lewin, K. M. (1998). Policy and planning of Physical Science education in South Africa: Myths and realities. *Journal of Research in Science Teaching, 35*(7), 729–744.

Ogunniyi, M. (1988). Adapting western science to traditional African culture. *International Journal of Science Education, 10*(1), 1–9.

Osborne, J., Simon, S., & Collins, S. (2010). Attitudes towards science; A review of the literature and its implications. *International Journal of Science Education, 25*(9), 1049–1079.

Price, J. F., & McNeill, K. L. (2013). Towards a lived science curriculum in intersecting configured world: An exploration of individual meaning in science education. *Journal of Research in Science Teaching, 50*(5), 501–529.

Rogan, M. R., & Grayson, D. J. (2003). Towards a theory of curriculum implementation with particular reference to science education in developing countries. *International Journal of Science Education, 25*(10), 1171–1204.

Rollnick, M., Allie, A., Buffler, A., Campbell, B., & Lubben, F. (2004). Development and application of a model for students' decision making in laboratory work. *African Journal of Research in Mathematics, Science and Technology Education, 8*(1), 13–27.

Taylor, N., & Vinjevold, P. (1999). *Getting learning right: Report of the President's Education Initiative Research Project.* Johannesburg: The Joint Education Trust.

Treagust, D., Chittleborough, G., & Mamiala, T. (2003). The role of submicroscopic and symbolic representations in chemical explanations. *International Journal of Science Education, 25*(11), 1353–1368.

Tuckey, H., & Selvanatram, R. (1993). Studies involving three-dimensional visualisation skills in chemistry. *Studies in Science Education, 21*, 99–121.

Van Berkel, B., Pilot, A., & Bulte, A. (2009). Micro–macro thinking in chemical education: Why and how to escape. In J. Gilbert & D. Treagust (Eds.), *Multiple representations in chemical education: Models and modeling in science education* (pp. 31–55). Springer.

CHAPTER 6

What Can Science Teachers Learn from the Wine Expert?

INTRODUCTION

My first encounter with Denzel was in the wine tasting room of Peppadew Wine Estate in the Simonsberg valley. Peppadew Wine Estate is part of the Stellenbosch wine route in the Western Cape.

When I saw Denzel, I jokingly asked, 'So what does a young black man like you do behind the counter in a wine tasting room?'

He replied, 'This is my job. Besides that, I am also the manager here. But why am I not surprise at your remark? Most people that visit us here normally give me a look that says, what do I (Denzel) know about wine? Until they discover how much I know.'

During my stay on the estate, Denzel and I often discussed the sensory properties of various wines. I was surprised and impressed by his passion for and immense knowledge of wine. He could identify all the different floral aromas and flavours of the wines I tasted, and he knew the history of the vintages.

In ignorance I asked, 'Why are you telling me all this, because to me all red wines taste equally awful?'

He said, 'Taste is but 20 % of a wine, while the remaining 80 % is presentation that has nothing to do with taste. If you pair it with the right food, the taste that you say is awful, might change. I also hated the taste of red wine at first, but then I learned how to identify all the different sensory properties of wine and my opinion changed.'

© The Author(s) 2017
O. Koopman, *Science Education and Curriculum in South Africa*,
DOI 10.1007/978-3-319-40766-1_6

At the end of my visit, I said to Denzel, 'Of all the different wine farms I have visited, this is by far the most informative and invigorative experience I have ever had in a wine tasting room. I always find it difficult to identify the different flavours that a wine offers, but today I came close to understanding it. How did you learn all this?'

He responded, 'I know it's not easy, but my senses guide me. This took me a long time to master.'

As I walked away reflecting on the experience and how much I learned about wine from Denzel, I realised that his knowledge of red wine was not something I could learn theoretically—knowledge of wine is deeply subjective and connected with the body and the self.

This brings me to the aim of this chapter. Firstly, this is a phenomenological narration of Denzel's childhood experiences, with a specific focus on the significance of (traumatic) events and experiences during his childhood and how these later influenced his choices in life. Secondly, the chapter aims to describe and explain how Denzel learned systematically to anchor the different sensory properties of wine in his mind. In the process, the chapter gives details of his embodied experience and shows that the body, or what Merleau-Ponty (1962) calls 'the sum part of the body', is essential in the learning process. Finally, the chapter highlights important lessons for science teachers from the lived experiences of the wine expert. Accordingly, the study draws from Merleau-Ponty's 'lived-body theory' to unpack how our everyday existence in time and space—that is, how events and situations in our life—shapes our thinking. He posits that we live in a world and our existence is tied to the space that we occupy. Broadly this means that our perceptual mindset correlates psychologically with our body as a whole in time and space. Next the chapter unpacks the role of a wine expert in restaurants and wine estates.

What Does a Wine Expert Do?

According to Dewald (2008), there are many descriptions of a wine expert or sommelier, as they are known in the restaurant trade. MacNeil (2001) describes the wine expert in a restaurant as someone who recommends wine to customers. The wine expert is also responsible for updating the wine inventory, training service staff in selling wine and assisting customers in selecting wine to accompany their meals. Aspler (1991) adds that a wine expert must keep abreast of consumer trends to help with the pairing of food and wine. As a result, the focus of the training of wine experts over the years has shifted from product knowledge, such as wine profiling, to assisting in the selling of wine that complements certain dishes. Dewald (2008) points out that although wine experts' main function is to increase wine sales in restaurants, they must also know how to pair the right wine with the right food. Market research has shown that product knowledge is key in the selling of wine and that many wine consumers' first experience of wine is guided by knowledgeable restaurant staff (Dewald 2008).

The role of wine experts on wine estates differs a little from their role in restaurants. Fountain et al. (2008) have found that wine experts on wine estates encourage return visits and they help in the establishment of wine clubs. They have an added advantage in that they can create an emotional bond between customers and their choice of wine. In other words, they assist in creating and developing brand loyalty for producers by making the wine tasting experience memorable. Therefore, it could be argued that the wine expert's role in the wine tasting room is to establish a relationship between the wine estate and the consumer and to initiate a concrete connection with the customer. Because it is important to create a relationship between the wine farm and the customer, wine farms incorporate this relationship between the wine expert and the customer in their strategies to boost wine sales (Ibid 2008). Establishing brand loyalty through wine tasting requires more than just good service—it also requires a personalised experience to encourage an emotional connection between the wine expert and the wine estate brand.

THE WINE TASTING EXPERIENCE

Approximately 7.924 million hectares of land were assigned to grape production worldwide in 2006 (Costa-Font et al. 2009). This figure increased by 0.8 % in the last decade. Almost half (i.e. 3.410 million hectares) of the entire grape production industry is located in European countries such as France and Italy. South Africa's grape farming constitutes 3.3 % of the global market; the country is the world's ninth largest wine producer. In South Africa winemaking is a fundamental part of the economic and social landscape of the Western Cape. World-class wines are produced in areas close to Cape Town, including Paarl, Stellenbosch and Worcester.

Table wines are constantly evolving, which means that their sensory properties continuously changes. Francis and Williamson (2015) point out that sensory tests may produce different results depending on the age of the wine when it is tested: the same wine may give different results when it is released and one to two years later. It is therefore accepted that the sensory properties of most sparkling and table wines change over time. In his book entitled *Making Sense of Wine Tasting,* Young (2010) draws attention to the art (or science) of wine and its evolving sensory properties. He echoes that although wine experts use their gifts of sight, smell, touch and taste in conjunction with brain function to determine the quality of a wine, their findings cannot be guaranteed; therefore, it is difficult to give an absolute definition of what 'a quality wine' is. However, this does not rule out the value and impact of oral stimuli as important determinants of wine quality (Pickering et al. 2010). Oral sensations are complex and depend on various factors such as ethnicity, age, gender and overall health in addition to other physiological factors (Pickering et al. 2010). Physiological factors, such as sensitivity to *6-n*–propylthiouracil (PROP) and bitterness, cause some individuals to perceive the taste and tactile sensations of red wine more intensely than others. These factors make the description of wine based on oral sensations even more challenging.

How Wine Tasting Developed in the Contemporary World: A Brief Literature Review

Historically, only expert winemakers and trained sommeliers were used to evaluate the quality of wines (Francis and Williamson 2015). These experts used a 20-point hedonic scale (explained below) to evaluate wine quality. Then researchers found that sensory characteristics were not part of the evaluation process and did not play a role in the rating of wine quality. Francis and Williamson (2015) write that the 20-point hedonic scale had many disadvantages, but the main one was that two different wines could receive similar ratings although they had completely different compositions. This caused farm owners and winemakers to turn to consumers for their input. Studies done in California in 1959 revealed that producers turned to consumers to rate the wine quality. The 20-point scale was reduced to a 9-point scale to assess the consumers' likes or dislikes. The nine-point hedonic scale was developed by David Peryam and his colleagues at the Quartermaster Food and Container Institute of the US Armed Forces and the University of Chicago in 1955 (Jones et al. 1955). The scale became the standard for measuring food quality and consisted of verbal anchors such as (1) like extremely, (2) like very much, (3) like moderately ... (8) dislike very much and (9) dislike extremely. The scale did not require wine tasters to concentrate on sensory properties to evaluate wine flavours, taste or texture; instead, it focused on verbal anchors that were unambiguous to the testing panel.

In an attempt to help wine producers to increase their sales, wine experts decided to include the levels of sweetness and bitterness in the scale. Prior to the year 2000, only experienced consumers who loved wine served on wine tasting panels. Inexperienced consumers were excluded because research had shown that chances were less than 5 % that inexperienced consumers and professionals would name the same wine as best in its class (Young 2010). Young also points out that professionals and inexperienced consumers used different criteria for what they considered to be a high-quality wine. As research progressed, it was found that a panel combining inexperienced consumers and trained experts would provide powerful sensory analytical data and practical insights into the rating of wine. Numerous studies have been done on sensory analytical data, such as specific wine texture, aroma, flavours and tastes, as provided by experts and consumers (see Yegge 2001). From 2001 to 2011 at least two papers per year were published on the sensory experiences recorded by wine consumers and experts (Fisher and Williamson 2015). It is apparent, according to Fisher and Williamson (2015), that the sensory science of wine tasting has a well-deserved place in wine research. Today, the views of expert wine tasters who quantify the sensory attributes of a set of wines are generally considered by the sensory science community as the best indication of consumer acceptance. Many studies have focused on the place of sensory data in wine tasting and how physiological factors impact on wine sensory data, but no study has yet investigated how knowledge of sensory '*data contributes to the knowledge*'. In other words, no one has yet studied how wine experts' existing knowledge of sensory properties is anchored in their mind and retrieved from their long-term memories to help them rate a wine accurately and reliably. This study hopes to determine whether these thought processes involve conscious and calculated reasoning or whether they just require the expert to be present in the moment. Although this study only involves one participant, it will provide baseline data for future studies.

THEORETICAL FRAMEWORK

Since the aim of this study is to recount Denzel's childhood experiences and to describe and explain how he systematically learned to identify and describe the sensory properties of wine, I will briefly discuss the different psychological theories of learning, namely behaviourism and cognitionism.

This will be followed by a succinct explanation of Merleau-Ponty's (1962, 2005) 'lived body' theory. It is important to unpack these psychological theories because we cannot deny their value and usefulness. Therefore, the study acknowledges the usefulness, strengths and limitations of behaviourism and cognitionism and draws on Merleau-Ponty's lived-body theory to describe and explain how Denzel systematically learned to understand the flavour profile of wine. The lived-body theory argues that the body consists of various parts and expresses learning through each part in a living connection in time and space (Merleau-Ponty 1962, 205).

The Theory of Behaviourism

The theory of behaviourism was first postulated in 1925 by the psychologist John Watson in his book entitled *Behaviourism* (Rabil 1967). Watson's theory, as noted by Rabil (1967), originated from a critique of empirical psychology in which he made Ivan Pavlov's data more meaningful. To Pavlov, psychological functioning could be explained from observed behavioural data. Such observable data led to a breakthrough and the proposal of a scientific methical structure to predict how organisms behave and subsequently learn. The term behaviourism covers three separate doctrines, namely (1) metaphysical behaviour (i.e. there is no such a thing as consciousness; there are only organisms behaving), (2) methodological behaviourism (i.e. true psychology can only study publicly observable behaviour and is not allowed to deal with introspection) and (3) analytical behaviourism (i.e. psychological concepts can be analysed exclusively in behavioural terms) (Rabil 1967).

The physiological basis of Watson's behaviourist psychology, according to Rabil (1967), is the theory of the reflex arch. He states that the reflex arch provides details of the various pathways that external stimuli follow into the body to cause a reaction. Firstly, he notes, an incoming stimulus is received by a sense organ, causing afferent neurons to transport the received stimulation to the central nervous system (CNS). Motor neurons then conduct the stimulation from the CNS to the effectors (a muscle or gland), resulting in a reaction. This process is extremely complicated because the stimulus and the reaction involve a number of reflex arcs that adjust the different reflexes to perform a co-ordinated action. From a behaviouristic perspective, the wine expert's learning about the sensory properties of wine can be explained in terms of the various pathways of taste sensations through the body. These involve nerves, neurons, nervous tissue and muscles (in the mouth and on the tongue) that cause sensations and reactions. These sensations and reactions are transferred via various neurons which connect the nervous tissue sending information through a series of excitation points through motor mechanisms. In other words, the body puts into action receptor apparatus that in turn puts into play a number of autonomous circuits. The winemaker experiences stimulus that is mechanistic in nature. Merleau-Ponty (1962) challenges this theory from two angles. Firstly, he points out that the body is the *sum total of parts* that are co-ordinated at every instant, and each part of the sensory apparatus is sensitive to only one form of stimulation. Secondly, the body is viewed as a passive agent that reacts and adjusts itself to external stimuli which act as causes. According to Merleau-Ponty (1962), this means that the body's response is similar to that of a dead object; therefore, there can be no distinction between man and the objects around him.

Cognitionism

In the 1960s the behaviourist view of learning lost momentum and was eventually abandoned in favour of cognitive theories of learning. Piaget (1960), a pioneer of cognitive learning, argues that cognition denotes structures that are internally organised wholes or systems of thought used as rules for the processing of information. As a result, learning takes place in cognitive isolation and is not informed by day-to-day contingencies of experiences within the social and cultural settings. Therefore, according to the Piagetian paradigm, learning is largely informed by interaction between the conceptual domains of the home, community and school. The introduction of cognitive learning developed into constructivism, which was further expanded to social constructivism (Vygotsky 1986), socio-cultural constructivism (Jegede 1999) and socio-cultural critical constructivism (Ogunniyi, 1988). 'Socio' means knowledge that is socially constructed; 'cultural' refers to the role of culture in the learning process, with specific reference to indigenous people and the knowledge they hold about the world; and 'socio-cultural critical' refers to critically reviewing the impact of 'social' and 'cultural' aspects on learning. These theories of learning have in common the notion that learning is a cognitive experience; they do not recognise that the 'whole body' participates in the learning experience. Constructivism views the world as an extension of the mind. To the wine expert, this means that senses play a minor role in the knowledge acquisition process as the emphasis is on information and the retention of that information. In other words, from a cognitive perspective, the understanding the sensory properties of wine can be described as an associationistic and inductive process. Consequently, the wine expert's mind becomes an extension of his body. Neither behaviourism nor cognitionism pays attention to the 'sum of the parts' of the body and its place in the knowledge acquisition process. This begs two questions: (1) When an individual is confronted with the task to identify and describe the sensory properties of wine, is it possible that the person can do so by using scientific data or is it a question that the mind can figure out on its own? and (2) Does the task require the individual to use the 'sum of the parts' of the body to provide a more truthful and accurate answer? In an attempt to answer these questions and to describe and explain the role of the body in the learning process, I now turn my attention to Merleau-Ponty's lived-body theory.

Merleau-Ponty's Lived-Body Theory

Merleau-Ponty (2005) posits that lived space is an existential space between the individual and the world in which he or she lives. He propounds that lived space is embedded in both time and space. To corroborate this claim, he writes, "The experience of our body teaches us to embed space in existence" (171). This statement implies that the body is tied to a certain world, and that world has an effect on the way a person feels. The person becomes the space he or she inhabits and the space becomes the person (Norlyk et al. 2013). Accordingly, lived space is an amalgam of the places, things, situations and events that give meaning to a person's existence. On this premise, the way we are connected to the world determines the meaning we give to the world (Merleau-Ponty 1962). Thus, perception takes place through the body which acts like a projecting instrument of our intentions in the world. So, we do not only perceive something with our eyes, our minds or any other bodily organ but also perceive things with the sum of the parts of the body.

In the lived-body theory, Merleau-Ponty (1962 and 2005) alludes to the essence and interrelatedness of being and the being. Being, as explained by Heidegger (1967), is synonymous with the German word *dasein*. To explain the meaning of the word *dasein*, Heidegger uses an idiosyncratic locution which is composed of *da*, meaning there (and/or here), and *sein*, meaning being, to exclude all other assumptions and prejudices of being, such as human being, man and homo sapiens. Merleau-Ponty

(2005) explains that being refers to a person that finds him or herself in a specific location (space), which when translated means being there or being in the situation. The being (the self) and being (in the world) form the two poles of Merleau-Ponty's thought (Rabil 1967). Indeed, Rabil (1967) echoes, "Neither the subjectivity of the self nor the objectivity of the world, but the relationship between them … continuously renders the self more than subjective and the world less than objective …" (viii). This statement points out the difference between the being in space (in a situation) and an object that is located in a container. An object in a container cannot connect with the space it occupies nor can it perceive other objects around it because objects do not have the gift of awareness that humans have. Spatiality for Denzel's childhood experiences cannot be informed by cognitive perceptions and beliefs. Instead, the perception of space (i.e. his childhood experiences on the farm) should be expressed through the 'totality of the life of the subject' (Rabil 1967, 296). Therefore, to perceive Denzel's body ontologically requires an understanding of his surrounding world during childhood. His childhood experiences bring with them a heightened state of awareness that can be represented as felt space or lived-through experiences that shaped his existence and mindset. Subsequently, the events external to his body and his perception thereof vary because 'there are two sides of a single act' (Rabil 1967, 211). To explain the single act, which represents a real event or an experience, I turn to Jasper's (1997) explanation of what a real event or felt experiences entail in order to locate Denzel's psychological connectedness to the space he occupied as a child and also to explain how he acquired an understanding of the sensory properties of wine.

According to Jaspers (1997), realness is an experience (of an event) at a specific time and place that is perceptually tangible in the lifeworld of a person. Moreover, a real experience is not an imagined or fictitious experience but a physical experience that is impressed on the mind as felt space (or awareness). This felt space is automatically retained in the mind as a memory. A real experience occurred at a specific time, in a specific place and for a specific duration and is stored as an episodic memory in the brain. When this happen the stage on (space in) which the event or experience has taken place changes from physical space to mental space. This shift from physical to mental space is in accordance with Plato's divided line where the real event that brings with it felt knowledge takes a cataclysmic turn to reach the intelligible realm called knowing. Thus, knowing is not the accumulation of information, but a recollection of bygone events that occurred at certain times and in a certain space. The constituents of knowing are copied from the physical events and experiences. Bringing this discussion closer to the wine expert's systematic learning of the sensory properties of wine, the real is concrete and represents a physical event that occurred at a particular moment. The tasting or drinking of wine is a mediation of a physical moment in a spatial dimension that becomes subsumed as part of the body and human liminality. It is through the parts of his body that he is connected to the various ingredients of wine and its various flavour sensations. Through the sum of the parts of his body, and more specifically the sense organs, the external is made implicit and is assimilated in the mind. In other words, his body is made explicit to the external, and he develops his perception through a process of self-awareness (or consciousness). When exposed to the same event at a different time and in a different space, the body surveys the mind in its entirety to retrieve felt experiences. The mind, therefore, becomes subordinate to the body as the senses help the body search for a new understanding from previous events and experiences of a particular phenomenon.

Conversely, an unreal event is predicated on a secondary experience derived from the lived-through experience or events experienced by others. An event experienced by others procures knowledge that is mechanistic and associationistic in nature because it has not been experienced personally in physical space. Secondary experiences generate knowledge that is a product of cognitive inquiry that is founded on information and not on awareness or personal lived-through experience. For example, winemakers record every detail of taste, flavour and various sensory properties of wine at different stages of the winemaking process. These experiences and observations are recorded in a wine manual and can be accessed by wine experts to predetermine what tastes and flavours to look for when they taste a wine. This act of wine experts is a cognitive act in which they aim to understand the flavour profile of wine. Therefore, what this study investigates from Denzel's lived world as a wine expert is not cognitive but rather how he embodies the knowledge of wine as real and felt space when he identifies and describes its various sensory properties.

The Research Approach

Since the aim of this study is to recount Denzel's childhood experiences and to investigate how he came to understand the various sensory properties of wine, Husserlian phenomenology as opposed to other phenomenological approaches is deemed necessary for the data construction process. Kvale (1983) points out that Husserlian phenomenology allows the researcher to zoom in on the phenomenon and to report it accurately and completely. Consequently, data was collected from two in-depth, open-ended interviews conducted from two different angles to elicit rich descriptions of Denzel's childhood and life as a wine expert.

THE INTERVIEWS

The interview questions were aligned with the main aim of this study, which was to delve into Denzel's consciousness to gather as much rich descriptive data as possible about his thoughts and feelings during his childhood. From this portraiture angle, the interview focused on questions such as how he ended up on the farm, where he was born and raised, his childhood experiences on the farm, his parents' role on the farm, the nature of his relationship with his parents, and how and where he spent his school holidays. These were followed by general questions relating to his beliefs, his feelings and his perception of wine during his childhood. The answers to these questions provided deep insight into Denzel's consciousness as a child and a teenager and its subsequent impact on his choice of career. At this stage of the interview, I remained mindful of Husserl's (1970) famous advice, namely that researchers should *return to the things themselves*, as well as Husserl's (1975, xix) dictum of the *epoché*, which is the notion to bracket out any pregiven or a priori standpoint. These aspects created a passageway into Denzel's *ideutic residuums* (i.e. subconsciously held ideas) (Ibid) to uncover the intentional acts of his life as a child.

The second part of the interview went beyond mere physical events and experiences and focused on how he acquired his knowledge of wine. This genealogical part of the interview revealed how he systematically came to understand the profiling of wine such as the bouquet and its unique sensory properties through rigorous inquiry and self-reflection. I focused on questions such as how he acquired his expert knowledge of wine and whether his skills came naturally or were learned theoretically? I wanted to determine how he brought a semblance of meaning and the significance of the multiple sensory properties of wine together as a unit. For example, I asked, 'Denzel, when you taste or drink red wine, what do you think about? How do you identify the different aromas and flavours in wine? How do you differentiate between the taste and flavour sensations? Are these aromas and flavours produced in your mind or do your senses connect with your body to develop your perceptions of the flavour profile? How long did it take you to acquire all this knowledge?'

The answers to these questions allowed me to determine whether his descriptions of the aromas and flavours were based on calculated reasoning or simply on a way of being or what Jaspers (1997) refers to as felt space.

ANALYSIS

In his doctoral thesis, Devenish (2002) adapts his data explication method from Schweitzer's model, which has been informed by Giorgi's (1985) model, in which the main themes are represented in a succinct and coherent manner. I used the model presented below to work with my raw data. My analysis was guided by Devenish (2002, 5), as illustrated below:

1. The researcher must have a sense of the whole interview. After the interview has been transcribed, the researcher must read and reread the transcript until he or she can identify the main ideas that point to some level of understanding about the crux of the research question.
2. The second step entails reading the transcript to reveal the core meaning that points towards the research question.
3. The third step involves the construction of key ideas with categories and subcategories that correlate with the research question.

I scrutinised the transcript of the interview with Denzel in search of descriptive and ontological clues to get an understanding of his world as a wine expert. From the transcript, I identified data that were informative in some way and highlighted important phrases and messages that were hidden. This involved an iterative process, which is a continuous back and forth movement between texts, as described by Devenish (2002). I followed this process until I was sure that I had sufficient information to answer my research question truthfully and accurately.

I paid careful attention to the language and terminology Denzel used, such as wine profiling, bouquet, vintage and acidity. At this stage, I tried to place myself in Denzel's shoes to live through his experiences in the hope of understanding what he said during the interview. This enabled me to understand how he thought and what he experienced when he performed the task of abstraction while creating a wine profile.

FINDINGS

The findings are divided into two sections. In the first section, I use Husserlian phenomenology to report on Denzel's experiences during his childhood, teenage years and early adulthood. Here I provide the data as transcribed, followed by a descriptive narrative using mostly Denzel's direct words, comments and expressions, as is customary in the phenomenological tradition. In the discussion section, I provide an interpretive narrative to give meaning to or to describe and explain his direct words and to separate the essential aspects from the peripheral. At this stage, I focused on Merleau-Ponty's (1962) lived-body theory in an attempt to explicate what Denzel intended to say during the interview. His responses are analysed and their psychological meaning investigated. The emphasis is on his childhood and his role as a wine expert and how his thoughts unfolded in his consciousness and brought him to an understanding of the various sensory properties of wine.

DENZEL'S CHILDHOOD

Here follow excerpts from the interview with Denzel about his childhood:

Interviewer: *Tell me more about where you were born and raised.*
Denzel: *I was born here on the farm. Both Mom and Dad started to work on the farm at a very young age and my grandfather [Mom's dad] introduced them to the farm. Mom was always working in the vineyard or in the farm owner's house. This gave me exposure to the farm owner's house while Dad was the foreman on the farm. Dad had to look after the general workers who worked in the vineyards.*
             I grew up very poor. My parents could not buy me things.
             Today I am actually a third-generation farm worker. As I became older, after school I would play in the vineyards, hit the vines to remove the snails that destroyed the vines ... From dad I learned how to work the soil and prune the vines. ...
Interviewer: *What was your view of wine as a young boy?*
Denzel: *As a teenager I used to hate wine and promised myself that I would never work on the farm. It was embarrassing to see how the people were talked down to. Also how many of the farm workers abused alcohol—especially my father. I said I would never touch alcohol because I did not understand how my father became addicted. It broke my heart as a child when I saw what wine did to my father and those that worked on the*

farm. When I visited the farm owner's son, while Mom cleaned their house, I saw a different picture of how they drank and enjoyed wine. I was exposed only to the bad side of wine and not the good side of it. My father and the farm workers would spend their entire salaries on wine and it destroyed them. This made me hate wine.

Interviewer: *How did the way the farm workers were treated and 'talked down to ...' by management made you feel?*

Denzel: *These injustices stood up in me and motivated to become someone better. I wanted to prove a point to the farm managers that I can do it. I did not know then that I will become a wine expert but I did rise above the expectation of many.*

Interviewer: *So what changed between your childhood and now because now you are a wine expert?*

Denzel: *Well, everything changed—the way I look at and understand wine today. My passion for wine was sparked by a young student who worked here in the wine tasting room, Renier. He was just so passionate about wine. That to me was the most amazing thing. I learned a lot from him as I watched carefully what and how he did things. The way he explained to customers how to identify the different ingredients of wine and how to match wine with food—it was different from how I perceived wine. I knew wine as a destroyer of relationships and the cause of violence. Every evening after work Renier would pour us a little wine to taste and asked us what we thought about it. At that stage wine tasted terrible, but since then I looked at wine differently.*

Interviewer: *When and where did you meet Renier for the first time?*

Denzel: *During school holidays I would work in the wine tasting room. That is where I met Renier for the first time. He worked behind the counter while I was responsible for buffing glasses, cleaning the floors and the toilet, pushing the heavy trolley with the wine to the car parking areas for customers. This is also where I was exposed to the business side of the farm.*

DISCUSSION

Denzel's Childhood and Teenage Years

Denzel grew up on the farm in abject poverty, with an alcoholic father that 'embarrassed him'. At a young age he learned about grape farming, although not formally. He describes how his father and the workers showed him how to prepare the soil and distinguish between the different soil types suitable for different grape cultivars used to make different wines. He learned how to throw 'buttons in the soil' and 'hit the vineyards to remove the snails that destroy the vineyards'. During school holiday, he earned pocket money by working in the tasting room, where he had to clean toilets and floors, buff glasses, push heavy trolleys to customers' cars, and so on. During this phase, Denzel was exposed to the business side of the farm. At that stage of his life he had a very negative perception of wine; he said, 'I hated wine, because I could see what it did to my father and the workers... It broke my heart to see what wine did to them...'

His negative perceptions of wine were reinforced through personal traumatic experiences as a child; he regarded wine as a destroyer of families and the cause of violent behaviour. Denzel recounted how his perceptions started to change when he observed a young student, Renier, behind the counter in the wine tasting room. He said, 'He was just so passionate ... since then I looked at wine differently...'

The events of Denzel's childhood and his experiences as a child gave meaning to his life and were incorporated into his consciousness. According to Todres et al. (2007), the events in a person's world have a number of potential meanings depending on where and how they fit into the person's lives. These things can have immediate and/or long-term consequences for the person.

According to Merleau-Ponty's (2005) lived-body theory, Denzel's childhood experiences on the farm may signify an indissoluble connectedness between him and the events on the farm. He experiences the traumatic events on the farm during so intensely as a child that those events formed the basis of his personality and individuality. Consequently, they shaped his concrete personal philosophy, giving rise to his belief and value systems. Denzel's heightened emotional state of awareness as child is expressed in the statement 'I hated wine'. This statement reminded him of the consequences and dangers of drinking wine.

Drawing from Merleau-Ponty's existential spatial analysis, it is a fair assumption that Denzel's body inhabited the traumatic events and conditions on the farm and the farm inhabited his body. This corroborated in the statements 'These injustices stood up in me ...' and 'I wanted to prove a point ...' These statements also reveal the spatial grip his childhood experiences had on his consciousness and therefore on his personal world or his reality. This spatial grip can be viewed from two perspectives: (1) the power the body has over certain actions and activities that cause the body to enjoy its space and (2) the grip that situations and events have over the body resulting in the event having power or control over the body. Merleau-Ponty (2005) points out that when we use our arms, hands, legs, eyes, noses, ears, and so forth, we learn more about the complexity of the world we inhabit. As a child, Denzel's negative perception of and attitude towards wine can be described as a crisis of the body triggered by lived-through or felt experiences. However, his mindset or perception of wine (that it is a destroyer of family life, causes violence, and so forth) changed when he observed Renier, who sparked in him a passion for wine. He explained this when he said, '...To me that was just the most amazing thing ... the way he explained to customers ... was different from the way I perceived it.'

The experience of watching Renier behind the counter enabled Denzel to find new meaning and to see new possibilities. Reiner's 'passion for wine...', Denzel explained, became a medium or a source that enabled him to see wine in a different light and transformed his hatred of wine into love. His interaction with Reiner brought about a change: wine as an object mediated a new space, and his old understanding and perceptions were replaced by new ones. His view that wine was evil was further transformed when Renier showed him that wine could also be paired with different foods to create richer and deeper enjoyment. According to Merleau-Ponty's (1962) lived-body theory, it is possible for the world of others to touch the depth of our lives.

In summary, the findings demonstrate a connectedness between the world of the subject and the conditions, situations, events and experiences on the farm. Firstly, there is shift from the world of the subject (Denzel) to the world on the farm. Secondly, this resulted in a unity between the human experience and the multiplicity of events. Thirdly, there is a dialectical understanding of the relationship between the past and the present, between the given and the novel experience.

How Denzel Acquired Knowledge of the Sensory Properties of Wine
Here follow excerpts from the interview with Denzel about his role as a wine expert and how he learned to describe the sensory properties of wine.

> Interviewer: *Do you have any formal wine-related qualifications?*
> Denzel: *When I was in Grade 12, I enrolled for a two-month short course at Elsenburg Agricultural College. I paid for it with the pocket money that I earned during holidays ... There I learned how to prune vines, but it was a very basic method they*

taught us. Today I know more about the methods that the viticulturist uses, such as canopy management. Later I enrolled at the Cape Wine Academy. There I learned the basics about wine and more about the history of South African wine. Then I did an advanced certificate to learn more about soil conditions, topography, north-facing or south-facing vineyards, field crafting, and so forth. I also did a certificate in international wines, the varietals and viticulture processes, and then I enrolled at the University of Stellenbosch for a course on wine evaluation that qualifies you to become a wine judge in South Africa. But most of these things I only did to get the formal qualification, because already I knew most of what the courses taught before I enrolled.

Interviewer: *So how did you end up behind the counter of the wine tasting room?*

Denzel: *After I had finished school I applied for the job, but did not get it. I set up a meeting with the owner and the managing director to inquire about the decision. He gave a long explanation that did not make senses. The long and short of it was that he picked up the phone, phoned the tasting room manager and told her I would start on Monday. That was a turning point for Peppadew wine farm. It turned from an all-white tasting room to a black and white tasting room.*

Interviewer: *Didn't you feel uneasy or scared when you first started working here? After all, what does a black man know about wine?*

Denzel: *True, at first I was very scared. The wine tasting room manager was not very happy. I wanted to prove to her that I could do it, so I started to study the wine manual of every wine.*

Interviewer: *What is a wine manual?*

Denzel: *The winemaker documents every step of the winemaking process. He records all the sensory properties of the wine as they change over time. He describes all the different aromas, floral flavours, fruitiness and various other things for research purposes. That was how I started to learn about all the wines.*

Interviewer: *Are you telling me that you learned these things through documents?*

Denzel: *Oh no, these documents were only a guide. Well, after work I would taste the different wines we offered to our customers. I would compare what I had read with what I tasted and vice versa. But this did not make me good at what I did in performing my tasks.*

Interviewer: *If the manual did not work, how did you then come to under-*
                  stand the sensory properties of wine?

Denzel: *I would buy different items, like peaches, liquorice, nuts,*
                  spices, and so forth. I would go home and sit for hours holding
                  each item close to my nose and then write down what I smelled
                  followed by tasting it until my brain remembered them, one
                  by one. I did this exercise many times. It helped me to become
                  good at my job, because I could easily identify the different
                  flavours.

Interviewer: *So how do you apply all of this when you taste or drink a wine?*

Denzel: *I no longer consult the manual. In fact, today as a wine judge*
                  I write the profile of a wine and it will not differ much from
                  what is in the manual. When I taste a wine, I know that each
                  wine is unique and has its own profile, although they come
                  from the same barrel. First, the presentation and aroma of a
                  wine are key. When I swirl the glass, it brings out the deep flo-
                  ral flavours and fruitiness of the different ingredients. When
                  I take the first sip, my senses are alive and the rest just comes
                  naturally. How do I know this? I don't know. But what I do
                  know is that I am seldom wrong when I describe or character-
                  ise a wine. Maybe I am just gifted. I don't know.

Learning as an Extension of the Body

Three things stand out in the transcript: Firstly, Denzel studied the wine manual to learn how to identify the various ingredients of wine and the taste sensations created. He claims that this cognitive approach 'served as a guide…' to help him understand the flavour profiles of wine. Secondly, he tasted different wines after work in search of the flavours recorded in the wine manual. Denzel claims that these cognitive constructions of knowledge did not help him much to identify and describe the various taste and flavour profiles required to be good at his job. His breakthrough in understanding the sensory properties of wine came when he decided to re-educate himself to use his senses. He said, 'I would buy different items like peaches, liquorice, nuts, spices, and so forth. I would go home and sit for hours holding each item close to my nose, and then write down what I smelled followed by tasting it until my brain remembered them, one by one.'

Merleau-Ponty's (1996) lived-body theory refers to this exercise as the intentional bow. When applied to this study, the intentional bow refers to the immersed being in search of clues to identify a pure object surveyed by the mind and sense organs co-ordinated by the different efferent nerves flowing through the body. Denzel had to separate himself from all preconceived, cognitively constructed knowledge from the past and involve his whole body to find absolute certitude. The aim of the intentional bow is not to explain objects in the world but to describe them in terms of their pure givenness as objects. This requires the observer to be present in the moment with heightened states of awareness to incorporate the properties and characteristics of the object into the body to become a habit of mind. In Denzel's case, a habit of mind was formed when the flavours and aromas of the different ingredients became embodied knowledge. Each time he intentionally smelled and tasted different ingredients, the incorporated knowledge blended with past experiences and events in his mind, and eventually, a habit of mind was formed. Denzel claims that a bodily experience unlocked the sensory properties of the ingredients. He said, 'I no longer consult the manual. In fact, today as a wine judge I write the profile of a wine and it will not differ much from what is in the manual.'

He confirms that a formal cognitive attempt to learn was not the answer when he says, 'But most of these things I only did to get the formal qualification, because already I knew most of what the courses taught before I enrolled.'

These words show that the knowledge was not based in the wine, in his mind or in his body—he had to learn to use his whole body to produce knowledge. In other words, the function of the body is not to know but to act. The action of the body in the world gives birth to knowledge at any moment in which the body exists.

WHAT CAN SCIENCE TEACHERS LEARN FROM THE WINE EXPERT?

I believe that understanding the way that a wine expert learns and masters his trade and skills can convey an important pedagogical point to science teachers specifically, as his learning involves mostly '[re]acting and doing' as opposed to learning 'about' wine. This is because the wine expert is actively involved in articulating his learning through practice, which requires him to join the dots on his own, so to speak. In other words, he did not learn to memorise concepts and theories about wine in order to understand it; instead, he learned from practice to develop his own theories of the flavour profile of wine. In particular, what separates his practice from formal learning is his appreciation of embodied knowledge derived from personal perceptual experience. The integrity of his perception is founded on the integrity of his bodily experience, which neither empiricism nor intellectualism recognises. Let's take a closer look at what we can learn from the wine expert's learning experiences that we can then transport to effective science teaching.

As I reflect on the wine expert's experiences and how he acquired his knowledge of the sensory properties of wine, numerous lessons for science teachers become evident, but I want to focus on two aspects: (1) the teaching and learning of science is a matter of '*doing*' as opposed to the traditional top–down authoritarian rote listing of facts. Just as the wine expert was '*consciously* and *actively*' attuned to his wine through his sense organs to unlock its sensory properties, so science teachers could encourage and guide their learners to use their senses to explore and understand their physical environment; (2) the wine expert's embodiment of knowledge about wine is a deeply subjective process that originates in and is made manifest though experience.

His purpose, desire and interest to understand the sensory properties of wine transport him from the narrow bounds of 'behaviourist and cognitive routines' to 'informal, unstructured and unfamiliar learning spaces'. This means his knowledge of wine has been assembled in ways that generate insights and information from constructing, deconstructing and reconstructing a phenomenon in a practical way. In this learning space, he not only assembles the '*what*', but along with the '*what*' he also learns the '*how and why*', which is different to the way that science is currently taught in schools. To do so, he has to train himself to use his senses not so much as instruments in search of some object, but to be directed and used in a *functional way*. This means he applies his senses for *practical end*s and *problem-solving* instead of as a means to an *end*. When the senses are used in a functional way, their true and real value is accentuated. So, instead of looking at an object for the sake of seeing and hearing it, the observer is consciously attuned to the object, with no predetermined objective as is common in school science practical work, but with an open mind that elevates him or her to a state of awareness that searches for details and clues like a scientists. Although the way he sharpens his connectedness to his senses for *functional* purposes is complex and difficult to articulate, it is his 'actions' (or methodology) that challenge the 'traditional approaches' of instrumental learning, which render the learner who perceives in the 'act' of perception as a 'passive' character or 'empty vessel' incapable of using his senses. Traditional approaches view the mind of the learner as a 'tabula rasa', that is an empty sheet that is disconnected from the body and consequently the senses. In this paradigm learning is reduced to a limited cognitive activity that entails the teacher writing notes or information on the brain of the learner. The wine expert's learning journey informs science teachers that experience is not blind and that it involves passive and receptive as well as active and constructive dimensions. As learners are guided to determine and understand the properties (i.e. nature) of different objects through a practical exercise, they can move beyond the confines of the purely conceptual and the imaginative to effective receptivity of their sense organs, which might allow the knowledge of science to become embodied. This embodied experience has the potential to take the learners to a state of awareness that could elevate them to self-understanding, which is in strong contrast to rote or memory learning.

If we reflect further, Denzel also expressed his admiration for and appreciation of Renier the 'inspiring character' that influenced his career trajectory. This illustrates the value and influence of an inspiring teacher. To explain the nature of the pedagogical relationship, for science teachers between Denzel and Renier, I will now draw on Frankfurt's (1988) philosophy. Frankfurt was concerned with what compels humans to act in accordance with what they care about, with what is important to them, and with what they love. This is because Frankfurt was driven by the question: What is it that moves people in making their choices and in their action? From this Frankfurt developed a notion of care as something that frames human action. To him this 'caring' is not simply about caring for others but rather with caring about or having a concern for something, which in this context refers to Denzel and Renier. Frankfurt came to the realisation that what people do and how they behave are guided by initiatives that are driven by a search for meaning. This search for meaning becomes the motivational force that makes people do things to give coherence to their lives. Denzel's admiration for Renier is rooted in his search for a more complete and fuller understanding of the self and his connectedness with growing up on the estate and with wine. This suggests that it is possible for learners to come to a fuller understanding of science if they pursue meaningful relationships with science teachers in ways that interest and drive them. Good science teaching has the potential to create motivational drives and desires in learners in such a way that they can give much more credence and value to the desire of their teachers than to their own. Drawing from Denzel's experiences, and corroborated by Frankfurt (1988), each encounter with a teacher is intelligible and should not be taken for granted. Cerbone (2006, 49) points out that our way of interacting with worldly characters as opposed to spiritual characters not only is some spatial containment to connote familiarity or involvement with others but represents a unitary moment in which learning takes place. From Denzel, teachers can learn that each moment is made up of antecedent intelligible components. In other words, even in each of those moments that learners are separated from the teaching environment, they are not entirely in solitude because their thoughts reflect on events and experiences that shape and influence them. As such, it is important to explore further this way of learning and doing in order to develop a more nuanced language to explain the learning spaces between teachers and their learners. Research has shown that in pedagogical practices, it is the relationship between teachers and learners that frames, shapes and sustains the learning process. Next, I explore what a wine expert's pedagogical approach to teaching might entail to unlock the mysteries of science for learners.

THE WINEMAKERS APPROACH TO DOING SCIENCE

Just as the wine expert's senses are closely attuned to the properties of wine such as the bouquet, colour, texture, fruitiness, tannins, sugar levels and acidity, learners should be encouraged to feel, touch, observe and taste the phenomena of interest to them. For example, since the rich chemistry of the orange (and many other fruits) forms part of the school syllabus, teachers can cut up different ripe and unripe oranges and distribute the pieces among two groups of learners to be carefully observed, touched, tasted and smelled to familiarise them with the physical properties of the fruit. They can be encouraged to look for the differences at the macroscopic level to understand the colour, texture, hardness or softness of the orange peels, their inside, as well as the viscosity, colour and taste of the juice. This can be followed up by comparing the acidity of each of the two oranges by performing a pH test. Based on their own experiences and hunches, the learners could explain how, in their opinion, the physical properties of the oranges are informed by their chemical properties; they could draw the molecular structures of citric acid, which is the main active ingredient of the juice. It is from this point onwards that they can be guided to identify the links between the chemical and physical properties of each of the two oranges and to compare the data of the ripe and unripe oranges in terms of their similarities and differences. Through such experiences, just as the wine expert is in touch with his or her grapes, the learner likewise connects through his or her rich sense organs not only to enjoy the orange but also to appreciate the chemistry of the fruit.

CONCLUSION

This chapter argues that learning is a complex activity that requires bodily action. Denzel's lived experiences as a child were influenced and shaped by the conditions and situation on the farm. According to Merleau-Ponty's (1962) notion of embodiment, Denzel became his environment. The conditions and hardships he experiences on the farm as a child shaped his way of being in the world. As a result, wine gained existential importance to Denzel. His exclamation '... I hated wine...' can be viewed as a true situation in which existence influenced wine and wine influenced existence. Hence, we learn that through the body we are in a living relationship to other bodies and objects, and the nature of this relationship gives meaning to our existence. This study highlights the complexity of learning. Although the findings reveal that knowledge travels through the body as an expression of the sum of the parts of the body, it also has elements of behaviourism and cognitionism.

Denzel's descriptions of the sensory properties of wine are a form of being acquired through habits of mind. This he achieved through constant exercise, experience or exposure to an event that embodies meaning. He experienced this embodied meaning through his eyes, ears, nose, tongue, and so forth, until it became an extension of his body. When the body becomes extended to the world, the world to which it is extended becomes true knowledge. Awareness of the body is not cognitive therefore, as Merleau-Ponty (1962, 231) puts it, "its inherence is never wholly clear or transparent." In conclusion, the body cannot be known at all except through the life we live in the world. Thus, the theory of the body is already a theory of perception.

REFERENCES

Aspler, T. (1991). Wine stewards a necessity or a luxury? *Foodservice and hospitality, 24,* 41–43.

Cerbone, D. R. (2006) Understanding phenomenology. Durham: Acumen Publishing Limited.

Costa-Font, M., Serra, T., & Gil, J. M. (2009). Explaining low farm-gate prices in the Catalan wine sector. *International Journal of Wine Business Research, 21*(2), 169–184.

Devenish, S. (2002). An applied method for undertaking phenomenological explicitation of interview transcripts. *The Indo-Pacific Journal of Phenomenology, 2*(1), 1–20.

Dewald, B. (2008). The role of the sommeliers and their influence on US restaurant wine sales. *International Journal of wine business research, 20*(2), 111–123.

Fountain, J., Fish, N., & Charters, S. (2008). Making a connection: Tasting rooms and brand loyalty. *International Journal of Wine Business Research, 20*(1), 8–21.

Francis, I., & Williamson, P. (2015). Application of consumer sensory science in wine research. *Australian Journal of Grape and Wine Research, Issue, 10*, 1–14.

Frankfurt, H. G. (1988). *The importance of what we care about.* Cambridge: Cambridge University Press.

Giorgi, A. (1985). *Phenomenology and psychological research.* Pittsburgh: Duquesne University Press.

Heidegger, M. (1967). *Being and time* (Macquarrie, J. & Robinson, E., Trans.). London: SCM Press.

Husserl, E. (1970). *The crisis of the European sciences and transcendental phenomenology: An introduction to phenomenological philosophy* (Carr, D., Trans.). Evanston, I.L: North-Western University Press.

Husserl, E. (1975). The Paris lectures, 2nd Edition (P. Koestenbaum Transl.). The Hague: Marthinus Nijhof.

Jaspers, K. (1997). *Psychopathology* (Hoenig, J., Trans.). Baltimore: John Hopkins University Press.

Jegede, O. (1999). Science education in nonwestern cultures: Towards a theory of collateral learning. In L. Semali & J. Kincheloe (Eds.), *What is indigenous knowledge? Voices from the academy* (pp. 119–142). New York: Falmer Press.

Jones, L. V., Peryam, D. R., & Thurstone, L. L. (1955). Development of a scale for measuring soldiers' food preferences. *Food research, 20*, 512–520.

Kvale, S. (1983). The qualitative research interview: A phenomenological and a hermeneutical mode of understanding. *Journal of Phenomenological Psychology, 14*(2), 171–196.

MacNeil, K. (2001). *The wine bible.* New York: Workman.

Merleau-Ponty, M. (1962). *Phenomenology of perception* (Smith, C., Trans.). London: Routledge and Paul Kegan (original work published in 1945).

Merleau-Ponty, M. (1996). *Phenomenology of perception* (Smith, C., Trans.). London: Routledge (original work published in 1945).

Merleau-Ponty, M. (2005). *Phenomenology of perception* (Smith, C., Trans.). London: Routledge (original work published in 1962).

Norlyk, A., Martinsen, B., & Dahlberg, K. (2013). Getting to know patients lived space. *Indo-Pacific Journal of Phenomenology, 13*(2), 1–12.

Ogunniyi, M. (1988). Adapting western science to traditional African culture. *International Journal of Science Education, 10*(1), 1–9.

Piaget, J. (1960). The general problem of the psychological development of the child. In J. M. Tanner & B. Inhelder (Eds.), *Discussion on child development* (Vol. 4). New York, NY: International Universities Press.

Pickering, G. J., Moyes, A., Bajec, M. R., & Decourville, N. (2010). Thermal taster status associates with oral sensations elicited by wine. *Australian Journal of Grape and Wine Research, 16*, 361–367.

Rabil, A. (1967). *Merleau-Ponty: Existentialist of the social world*. New York: Columbia Press.

Todres, L., Galvin, K., & Dahlberg, K. (2007). *Lifeworld-led healthcare: Revisiting a humanizing philosophy that integrates emerging trends*. Boston, MA: Kluwer Academic Publishers.

Vygotsky, L. (1986). In A. Kozulin (Ed.), *Though and language*. Cambridge, MA: MIT Press.

Yegge, J. M. (2001). Influence of sensory and non sensory attributes of chardonnay wine on acceptance and purchase intent. Unpublished doctoral thesis, University of California, Davis, USA.

Young, A. (2010). *Making sense of wine tasting: Your essential guide to enjoying wine* (5 ed.). San Francisco, CA.

CHAPTER 7

Harnessing the Full Use of the Senses in the Science Classroom

INTRODUCTION

According to Dewey (cited in Wong and Pugh 2001, 319), the goal of school science is to assist learners in understanding the world in order for them to lead lives rich in worthwhile experiences. To this end, school science should take learners beyond the abstract world of concepts, definitions and theories to *'an experience'* of the world in order to develop and extend their *ideas* about the world. *'An experience'* (to Dewey, cited in Wong and Pugh, 2001) is often misrepresented by many scholars who associate it with everyday events and occurrences in the lives of learners. This interpretation of everyday experience is "too casual and sporadic to carry with it any important implications for the nature of *nature*" (Dahlin 2001, 453). Dewey propagate 'an experience' as a unifying liberating moment that occurs between a person and nature in which all the elements flow, "without seam and without blanks", into what develops into an idea (Wong and Pugh 2001, 320). This means *an experience* is a knowledge-producing moment which the learner holds in his mind with some kind of apprehension or awareness. This form of learning and knowing is different from what is happening in schools today, where learners are subjected to memory routines and rote listing of facts. At the heart of Dewey's notion of *'experience'* is ascertaining how knowledge comes about through an active engagement with nature that is inspired by purpose, interest and desire. In other words, genuine educational moments

© The Author(s) 2017
O. Koopman, *Science Education and Curriculum in South Africa*,
DOI 10.1007/978-3-319-40766-1_7

involve the active engagement of the learner with the *concrete physical world* that results in the formulation of new *ideas*. Dewey explains the concept of *'idea'* as being synonymous with the "end product of a scientific inquiry" (cited in Wong and Pugh 2001, 322) in which the scientists deconstruct, construct and reconstruct existing knowledge leading to new perceptions. Thus, conceived, genuine learning of science is primarily the conjoining of *'an experience'*, criticality and active thinking.

Joseph Schwab (1959), in agreement with Dewey, believed that the true learning of science lies in the cord that binds experience, criticality, thinking and the theories of science. When the cord that binds these aspects is missing, learning becomes moribund. To bring these aspects together, one of Schwab's (1959) teaching techniques was to translate the scientist's theory or ideas into practice by asking, what is Newton's or Boyle's law *'doing'*? He was not interest in the accurate description of Newton's or Boyle's law; what mattered to Schwab was how the learner could apply Newton's and Boyle's laws in his or her personal life situations in order to elevate the learner's thinking to much higher levels of understanding. In other words, he encouraged critical engagement with the scientist's work by relating it to their personal lived world instead of blind repetition of the content. This is because in Schwab's view in science theory is secondary and is implicit in practice. This is predicated upon his belief that knowledge or information about the world did not start with concepts, laws and theories but has its origin in and through practice.

Schwab's discourse of 'doing' science and Dewey's epistemic precondition of 'an experience' requires the cultivation of careful and exact attention to all the qualities inherent in sense experience. Both agree that all knowledge in science is rooted in the sense organs as both want to move away from the dualistic Cartesian preoccupation with the mind. In other words, the learning of science is not a function of thought but is constructed through the use of the senses meticulously applied in the real world and converted into thought. This implies that the process of learning is unique and meaning is generated through what the learners see, touch, smell, taste and hear as an intrinsic criticality. This intrinsic criticality arrived at in experience makes learning not child-centred but 'experience-centred'. To corroborate this, McEwan (2010, 131) propounds that, without the use of the senses, one cannot gain meaning that goes beyond the purely practical and technical. He writes,

You cannot put knowledge into a soul that does not possess it, or sight into a blind eye. However, the soul of every man does possess the power of learning the truth and the organ[s] to see it.

Locke (2009) agrees and asserts that it is only through sense experience that one arrives at a full understanding of the environment, the surrounding world or the phenomena in it. Without it, humans lack knowledge. Locke argues that the individual's senses penetrate deep into the mind, creating several distinctive perceptions based on the properties of things as experienced in nature. Norris (1987, 775) avers that in science even the instruments that scientists use are dependent on the senses, and without them science has the potential to become 'less good or less worthy'. In other words, the learner's educational experience would consist of the accumulation of scientific facts without developing compelling ways of incorporating worthwhile experiences that can transport the learner beyond knowledge and skills.

This chapter aims to answer the following questions: (1) What value do the sense organs bring into the science classroom? (2) How can science teachers use the sense organs to push learners beyond the rote performance of scientific actions and processes to purposeful knowledge construction? In what follows the study will firstly provide a succinct overview of the state of science teaching and learning in South Africa. By drawing on the work of Heidegger (1967, 2002) and Locke (2009), I then discuss learning and the senses to unpack how the senses lead to sense making. This will be followed by an exploration of the discoveries made by several luminaries in the sciences and the role the senses played in these discoveries. Finally, the chapter outlines some strategies that science teachers can follow to encourage learners to actively engage their senses in the processes of knowledge construction.

THE CURRENT STATE OF SCIENCE TEACHING AND LEARNING IN SOUTH AFRICA

Approximately 25 % of South Africa's national budget is allocated to the education sector. This percentage amounts to roughly 25 billion rand per year spent on education. In an attempt to improve the quality of teaching and learning of science, the Department of Basic Education (DBE) launched the Dinaledi Schools Project in 2001 in an attempt to give specific and targeted support to selected historically disadvantaged schools. This assistance came in the form of huge monetary support to selected schools, where new laboratories were build and extra science and mathematics teachers were appointed to achieve more manageable learner–teacher ratios. This monetary support is predicated on the assumption that a high-quality science education programme is regarded as a good indicator of economic success around the world (Hanushek et al. 2008). Baker et al. (2002), in agreement with Hanushek et al. (2008), show through their research findings that there is a direct correlation between good performance in science and economic growth. To this end governments invest heavily in their school science programmes to monitor and improve its quality.

Yet despite heavy investment in mathematics and science teaching, in 2015 the World Economic Forum report rated South Africa as the worst performing country in learning mathematics and science (Muller 2015). Moreover, between 1995 and 2002, South African learners showed no improvement in the annual Trends in International Mathematics and Science Study (TIMSS) (Spaull 2013). Between 2002 and 2011 the TIMSS results revealed that the South African learners' performance was still poor in comparison to other countries (Reddy 2006). In 2003, South Africa was ranked last in science out of 49 countries that participated in TIMSS (Martin et al. 2004). Closer inspection of the TIMSS results (for South African learners) shows that three quarters of the learners had not acquired the minimum set of scientific skills. In addition, less than 1 % of the entire school science populace performed at an advanced level compared to the international average of 3 % *(ibid.)*. The poor performances of developing countries in TIMSS has often been attributed to many factors, of which Reddy (2006) found infrastructure and teacher quality to be the most important. This is particularly true for South Africa, he claims, given the legacy of apartheid, which resulted in the unequal distribution of resources. Fleisch (2007), in agreement with Reddy (2006), shares this view but argues that although the reasons are variable and highly complex, factors such as the socio-economic status of learners, teachers' CK, pedagogical knowledge, geographical locations and most importantly the language of teaching and learning are the main determining factors. Le Grange (2015, 8–9) puts the impact of the socio-economic factor on learner achievement in science in context when he writes,

> The most significant factor influencing educational achievement is socio-economic status. This is a composite variable. If you are poor you are likely to perform poorly at school, dropout of school and if you are fortunate to complete schooling, you will pass with poor grades or would have taken subjects

that will not give you vertical mobility into higher education or meaningful employment. If you are poor you will not have access to books, computers and other resources at home; your parents will have very little formal education; your school will be poorly resourced; many of your teachers will be under-qualified, your body will receive insufficient nutrients creating health risks such as disease, and so on. If you are poor and from a rural area then access to vertical mobility is reduced even further. The opposite is true for those who are affluent … South Africa reflects a bimodal system: a sub-system of learners from materially poor backgrounds who underachieve in schools and a sub-system of learners from materially privileged backgrounds who perform well at school.

Kenzani and Onwu (2013) found that teachers continue to fail to excite and attract learners to engage with the subject meaningfully. The reasons for this state of affairs are as follows: (1) the subject is taught as a rote listing of facts that learners find inappropriate and meaningless to their personal lived world; (2) teachers fail to bring their learners to an awareness of the social impact of science with particular reference to the rewards imbedded in the subject such as science's potential beneficial effect on personal development; (3) science teachers lack effective teaching approaches that link the content to the day-to-day lived experiences of learners, which is likely to further obscure and diminish the relevance of the subject in their lives. Studies conducted by Onwu and Stoffels (2005) and Dube and Lubben (2011) highlighted the poor quality of science teaching and the lack of effective teaching strategies, leading to poor understanding of the subject matter by learners. Le Grange (2015) argues that poor teaching as a result of poor teacher CK applies particularly in poor and rural communities. The language of instruction is another important factor that influences learners' understanding of science. Although there is a paucity of studies of this matter, he suggests that children who are given instruction in their mother tongue but who are assessed not in their home language perform significantly more poorly than those assessed in the same language as their mother-tongue teaching. Perhaps the latest 2015 National Senior Certificate results for physical science with a pass average of 58.6 %[1] is evidence of this, seeing that the majority of the students write the examination in a language that is not their mother tongue. These results also suggest that despite reform initiatives, quality educative experience in science remains below the ideal (Umalusi 2015). Many studies conducted over the last decade into the way science is taught show that scientific discourse and worthwhile educational experiences escape the learners as teachers rush through the syllabus to prepare learners for the final examinations (Reddy 2006; Sadler 2009).

Muwanga-Zake (2008) found that teachers devote little attention to practical work and learners have to endure boring chalk-and-talk lesson. In visits to numerous schools he found that although teachers have well-resourced laboratories that are fully stocked with chemicals, they do not do practical work because they feel inadequately trained to do so. As a result, the instruments, apparatus and chemicals collect dust in the storerooms. If practical work is done, it is only to confirm what is known (Muwanga-Zakes 2008). In practical work the main challenge learners face revolves around the dogmatic domination of settled hierarchies of knowledge and knowing that determine what learners should see and hear. These predetermined objectives 'bracket out' the use of the learners' senses, resulting in the reinforcement of memory routines (Mji and Makgoto 2006). Consequently, the value of practical work becomes questionable as learners merely confirm or illustrate the theories of science without any interrogation or in-depth critical engagement with data that could result in new understandings. This mode of doing practical activities embodies a cookbook approach in which learners follow instructions like a recipe handed down to them by teachers, without a clear sense of their practical implications and purpose (Hattingh et al. 2007). Koopman (2013) found that factors such as the lack of time, large class sizes and poor teacher training impinge on the teachers' practice in the science laboratories and classrooms. This raises the question: How can the current unsatisfactory state of science teaching be reversed in South Africa?

Although there is a paucity of empirical studies on the value of the senses in the teaching and learning of science, many science education researchers agree on its value (Donnelly 2004; Dahlin 2001; Øostergaard et al. 2008). This chapter offers, as an alternative discourse, an argument for the use of the senses in the science classroom. What I will attempt to show in the next section is the need for the use of the senses in doing science to break away from the theoretical discourse that alienates the learners not only from science but also from understanding nature and what science has to offer.

Learning and the Senses

In his philosophical thinking Heidegger (1967, 2002) was committed to *'lived experience'*. From his *commitment to lived experience* we learn it is a well-known fact that the knowledge people hold is almost entirely derived from their interaction with 'concrete physical things' in their immediate lifeworld (*ibid*, 58). This interaction leads to a sense-making process which promotes learning. During this sense-making process, individuals learn to classify objects as beautiful, ugly, colourful, interesting, or boring, among others. Each object is classified according to specific criteria, which would be impossible without the use of the senses. It is through the sense organs that the human body collect 'raw data'. This raw data is processed and rework to develop a perception. For example, it is through the senses that the observer becomes aware of the beautiful intrinsic or extrinsic properties of certain objects. The senses precede the mathematical because mathematical formulated physical laws are seen as observed phenomena that is considered more real than what is expressed through equations (Dahlin 2001). Husserl (1970, 48–49) writes of a

> surreptitious substitution of the mathematically substructed world of Idealities for the only real world, the one that is actually given through perception, that is ever experienced and experienceable—our everyday life.

Any scientist would unhesitatingly accept that the validation of scientific theories depends on evidence. By implication, then, the testing or verification of a theory is directly dependent on immediate sense experience. If experience is excluded, where will the proof or data come from? Locke (2009) endorses this idea: that is, it is only through experience that scientific theories become meaningful and through which objects become cognisable or identifiable. This identification of objects, which requires the effective application of the senses, provides the 'data' that individuals use to frame their ideas. As individuals experience different objects, challenges and stimuli or make observations, they learn to compile their own rule book of how they think the world works around them.

The development of this rule book of science through experience, according to Pickering (1995), is not straightforward as nature does not simply freely 'gives' facts and information to scientists or observers. Instead, the scientist have to work hard to collect evidence, from which they develop knowledge claims to accurately describe the natural world. Understanding the processes of science for theory building requires scientists to apply their senses in a functional way to see and hear for a practical end and problem resolution to produce evidence (Norris 1987). The collection of evidence involves describing objects and phenomena in ways that make things visible to the scientist and to others. This requires scientists to develop protocols, which in turn requires the use of the appropriate instruments, and so forth, to measure phenomena (Goodson 1994; Knorr-Cetina 1999). Once scientists have generated data through various experiments and investigations, they draw on theories to decide what to pay attention to by separating key aspects from the peripheral. In other words, theory determines how they describe their data and how to present this to others in the scientific community to elucidate their findings (Pickering 1995; Roth and Bowen 2001). These findings have the potential to result in knowledge claims which, Norris (1987) notes, require careful observation and dissection. The precision and accuracy of the findings become impossible without the use of their senses, that is, sight, smell, touch, taste and hearing linked to a sixth sense, namely intuition. Indeed, Norris (1987) argues that to the scientists sense perception is the key to understanding the physical world and the processes in it. They use their senses carefully to dissect for ontological clues.

Like the scientist, children are born with an inborn curiosity to understand how the world works. From various games and leisure activities children develop an understanding of the various scientific properties of objects. For example, when *observing* an everyday event such as throwing a ball or a stone into the water, they *realise* that a ball floats and a stone sinks. This experience becomes permanently fixed in memory because the external manifestations or empirical data of the phenomenon become part of their perceptual mindset. Although children observing such an event may not be familiar with the concept of buoyancy, the experience has the potential to transport them beyond the narrow bounds of what they observed. They might start to question the differences in the molecular composition of the respective objects, which might prompt them to conduct further investigations. Thus, knowledge not only becomes an act of seeing but a way of registering the experiential world around them. In other words, experiences, as illustrated in the example of throwing different objects into water, can be taken as raw data or 'lived through' generated by the senses that become the foundational evidence and start of the development of scientific theories. The distinction between what can and cannot be perceived by our senses is what drives the epistemological interest in the construction of knowledge.

Heidegger's (1967) philosophy of existence as opposed to other philosophies provides a description of how human knowledge in particular assists the individual in understanding something. He argues that any experience can translate into an idea that individuals use to navigate their way in nature. At the heart of this philosophy is the use of the senses as scientific instruments that enable individuals to *see* and to use that knowledge to find their way around in their immediate lifeworld. According to Heidegger (2002, 116), seeing is the ability to comprehend exact similarities and differences between objects. Furthermore, seeing is a way of making the *seen* object explicit by holding it in view so that it is manifest in such a way that nothing is hidden from it. This implies that the fundamental function of the senses is to reveal that which is hidden. In any environment, children learn to characterise, codify, analyse and draw inferences naturally by exploring the environment within which they live. The more individuals discover things themselves, the more comprehensively they learn to understand the principles of science in which things are rooted. In so doing, they learn to think and perceive their connectedness with nature through their own experiences with their surrounding lifeworld. Husserl sums up the experience of interacting with the environment through the senses as follows: "I am, I think, I live" (1975, 10). Through experience individuals learn to discover their true selves and understand their existence in the world.

Heidegger (1967, 78–82) points out that 'being in the world' is a compound expression for *dasein*. He argues that being in the world must be looked at in three different ways: firstly, being in the world denotes the quest to understand the ontological structure of the world; secondly, the question of *who* is in the world signifies the quest to understand the identity of the being who is present in the word; thirdly, 'being-in' (*Insein*) is the search for 'in-hood' (*Inheit*). He describes in-hood as being in the world, which represents the space that the being is in to negotiate meaning and understand the world. Linked to the world of the learner, the act of placing learners in a classroom to study science without using their experience as a point of reference is tantamount to removing an animal from its natural habitat, placing it in a cage and then expecting it to respond instinctively. Often learners are confronted with unfamiliar scenarios in the science classroom and expected to make sense of the information imparted to them in the course of a discussion. This type of teaching approach could have epistemological, pragmatic and methodological implications: *epistemological,* because the child's memory is disconnected from the information and therefore cannot internalise it; *pragmatic,* because the child has no sense data about the event to retrieve from memory and *methodological,* because his or her senses are not engaged in the classroom. Regarding my own experiences as learner, I can recall few instances in the science classroom where I was made to realise that there was more to the content than I actually thought there was. Consequently, instead of teaching me the art of using my senses to understand phenomena in the science classroom better, science became a battleground for rote learning and reciting definitions and abstract information.

Based on his experiences as a science teacher over a period of more than 50 years in Germany, Wachenscheim concludes that science teachers ignore the use of the senses in the science classroom and need to give urgent consideration to revising their teaching approaches:

> I knew that many school children have to suffer lessons in physics that scarcely let them recognize this as the science of nature. Instead, the phenomena of nature are hardly touched upon... paralysed in a condition as mere spectators that cannot be physically present with their senses, and for this reason they are also unable to perform the task of abstraction (cited in Østergaard et al. 2008, 93).

Reflecting on the teaching practices of science teachers up to 1975, Wachenscheim concludes that during that time teachers appeared to have dulled the enquiring minds of learners into a mute acceptance of scientific facts as if the latter were removed from their senses. He views the teaching of science during his long teaching career as little more than a static collection of facts, formulas and mathematical manipulations. Similarly, almost 30 years later, Donnelly (2004) expresses similar concerns about this instrumentalist approach to the teaching of science, which he attributes to science teachers being more concerned with knowledge *about* science than with *how* learners experience science on a daily basis. The knowledge teachers deliver to learners is often in conflict with the meaning-laden everyday experiences of learners. For the most part, creativity is replaced with regimentation, open-mindedness with conformity and higher-order critical thinking with the rote listing of facts.

Next, I discuss the role of the senses in the development of scientific theories.

SCIENCE AND THE SENSES

The past three to four centuries witnessed the appearance of several science luminaries responsible for a number of unprecedented discoveries in the domains of physics, chemistry, biology, medicine and astronomy which signalled a fundamental shift in the various ideas about how the world works. A feature these scientists had in common was an encyclopae-dic knowledge of science derived not from a textbook but from their con-nectedness with nature through the senses. For many centuries the sense organs were one of the main scientific instruments of investigation and provided a sphere of awareness that assisted researchers in understanding the scientific forces of the universe. I will now discuss the discoveries made by Lavoisier, Boyle, Galileo, Newton, Dalton and Mullikan and the role the senses played in their discoveries.

Learners are made to believe that scientists never fail and are seldom wrong. But in reality this is not how scientists work; what all these lumi-naries of science had in common is that they all failed countless times before arriving at conclusive evidence to prove their theories. In the eigh-teenth century, Antoine Lavoisier's *observation* of the calcination[2] of tin (Tn) in a sealed glass tube introduced the law of the conservation of mass, which initiated a revolution in chemistry. Cohen (1985, 236) writes, "It is evident that Lavoisier's chemical revolution passes all the tests for a revolu-tion in science." Lavoisier's main finding was derived from *observing* how tin burned in a sealed glass jar. After careful measurement, he concluded that the mass of the mixture of the gases remained constant. Similarly, Robert Boyle's preoccupation with heating substances over a flame led him to observe that different substances burn with different colours, which made him realise that it is the unique chemical properties of each substance that causes it to burn with different colours. This observation and conclusion contributed to the arrangement of the elements on the periodic table according to their unique properties such as colour changes when heated. For example, all elements in group one and two burns with a different colour flame when heated. Both Lavoisier and Boyle used their senses to perform the task of scientific abstraction and to synthesise, cod-ify and interpret phenomena. They built their own scientific instruments to measure and weigh objects and rooted their knowledge of science in their experience with phenomena by touching, smelling, tasting and, most importantly, seeing them. Jardine (1992) claims that any inquiry, in which the use of the senses is either denied or objectified, is deluded. It results in science purporting to be some dispassionate "fundamentum" (logical basis) in terms of which learners see science as a highly rational exercise with little internal epistemic drive or desire to understand it.

Galileo made major contributions to the field of physics, astronomy and mathematics. He studied the motion of objects in the gravitational field of the earth in the assumption that the earth was flat. This principle allowed him to study the acceleration of objects independently of where you place them and independently of their mass. As a resident in Pisa, where he lived for many years, he dropped different objects with different masses from the leaning tower of Pisa. He is famous for the apocryphal story of dropping a cannon ball and a feather from the same height above the tower. He observed that both objects fall in the same way at constant acceleration independent of their mass. From this observation he developed the equivalents principle, which explains that gravity is equivalent between all different objects independent of their mass. Isaac Newton, one of the greatest scientific minds of all times, is often described as someone who was in touch with the cosmos through the questions he continually asked about the natural world. One of the highlights of his life, often told by himself, was *seeing* an apple falling from a tree and the moon in front of him (Chabata 2013, 11). He realised that both objects (the apple and the moon) are in the same sphere and subject to the same gravitational force, except that the apple falls to the ground whereas the moon remains orbiting. He connected the two phenomena and ascertained that the speed at which the moon falls is fast enough to overcome the gravitational pull of the earth and allow it to continue to orbit. On the basis of this observed event, Newton invented calculus to prove that the cosmos is heliocentric. The heliocentricity of the cosmos has its origin in the work of both Galileo and Keppler, and when Newton connected these ideas, he realised that the same force (gravity) that makes projectiles move and fall to the earth is the same force that keeps the planets in orbits around the sun in the sky. From this observation he concluded that the earth is heliocentric. Newton also shone natural or white light through a prism and discovered that white light breaks up or splits into the seven different colours of the rainbow and vice versa, which refuted the prevailing belief at the time that colours were modified forms of white light. From this discovery, Newton deduced the laws of optics. Each of Newton's discoveries was based on close and thoughtful observation. It was this passionate sensory connectedness with the universe and inborn curiosity that prompted his theories about the world.

In 1893, John Dalton, another scientist who is often described as a genius by many of his peers (see Bryson 2003), suggested that there was more to the atom than what was known at that time, but his ideas remained unexplored and sounded absurd to many eminent scientists. At that time many scientists believed that there were no such things as atoms, and in response to Dalton's suggestion, Ernst Mach wrote, "Atoms cannot be perceived by the senses … they are things of thought" (cited in Bryson 2003, 179). Four years after Dalton's death in 1897, Thomson discovered the electron, which he *observed* through a microscope. In a paper published in 1897, Thomson described a number of experiments he performed in a cathode ray tube in search of the electron, which he referred to as a corpuscle (John Stoney is acknowledged as the person who named the electron). Thomson makes specific reference to 'seeing' whether there might be a chance of detecting the deflexions of the cathode rays by an electrostatic force. Thomson's observation was that the deflexion was proportional to the difference in the potential between the plates. Although the cathode ray was not visible to the naked human eye, Thomson claimed that he observed the deflexions of the cathode rays as they hit the phosphorescent screen at the end of the tube. The instruments used by Thomson made it possible to make the observation. This discovery led to the further development of theories of Newtonian physics, thermodynamics and classical electromagnetism. From this discovery of the atom, scientists could construct a whole new description of what the universe consisted of. Furthermore, they could understand and explain Faraday's notion of magnetic flux more accurately by grasping the connection between electricity and magnets, as well as the nature of the electricity of the magnet itself. Today, virtually everything owes its ideas and theories to this discovery or observation.

Ever since the discovery of the electron, new models of the atom have been proposed by researchers such as Rutherford, Bohr, Marsden and Geiger (see Feynman et al. 1965). Einstein built on their ideas and formulated his *special theory of relativity* to refute Newton's equation of motion, which had held sway for more than 200 years (Feynman et al. 1965, 151). Although Newton discovered the gravitational pull on objects, he could not explain what causes the objects subjected to gravity to be pulled downwards. It is said that as Einstein was standing at his office window, he had a vision of a man falling from the top of the building he was looking at. He realised that as the man was falling he is weightless and it is not gravity that is pushing or pulling the man down, but the earth that has curved the space (as in planetary bodies) around the man and that this curved space above the man that is pushing him down. From this he developed a new theory of gravity, which he called a new theory of the universe referred to as the special theory of relativity, because it only dealt with objects moving at constant speed. Today, this theory is used to put satellites into orbit and for global positioning systems, to name a few.

Robert Mullikan's contribution relates to the value of the elementary charge of electrons and protons. Mullikan sprayed perfume atomiser through a slit in the metal-charged plates to measure the settling velocity of the particles by carefully changing the intensity of the radiation and charges between the plates. He then shone light energy radiation on the particles to create charges on the neutral oil drops by turning them into ions. Once they (oil drops) charged, he charged the plates. He then observed the whole experiment through a telescope. His aim was to measure the settling velocity of the charged particles by changing the intensity of the radiation and charge between the plates. He observed that the distribution of the velocities is non-continuous, from which he determined that the electron charge is quantised and ascertained the elementary electron charge. By doing so, he could mathematically calculate the charge on the electron. It was the observations he made through his telescope that led him to the discovery of electronic charge. Significantly, the instruments which brought most of these scientific discoveries and laws to light were a combination of the senses, carefully designed experiments, and careful observations and measurements. Ever since then scientists have increasingly been expanding on the effective use and application of the human sense organs by inventing better microscopes, hearing aids, and so forth.

Nowadays, many decades later, science learners and university students are being kept busy with classroom activities that do not encourage the development of new ideas or discoveries but simply confirm the known without the careful use of their senses. Perhaps this is why Dewey (in McEwan 2010) proposes that the starting point of any lesson should not take the standard conventional form of imparting ideas and theories to the learner but should centre on discussing the results of experiments and observational assignments that address the burning issues that learners raise about the observable phenomena in nature. Dewey points out that those burning issues and unexplained phenomena—for example, why birds and aeroplanes can fly—should be used to ignite the learner's interests and should be at the centre of science teaching that engages all the learner's senses as investigative tools in the pursuit of knowledge.

Teachers should train learners at an early stage not to be scared of getting things wrong during investigations but to investigate phenomena by designing thoughtful experiments to validate or refute hypotheses. In so doing, teachers would affirm the learners' passion for asking questions and thus become co-inquirers with them. Teachers could also use the burning issues that learners raise in the classroom as a platform to develop lesson plans and classroom activities to stimulate critical thinking. These approaches to the teaching of science have the potential to stimulate a deep interest in scientific enquiry and knowledge per se and not merely acquire knowledge *about* science in general as learners learn to reflect on their experiences. Therefore, instead of focusing on scientific correctness, learners should be allowed to free their imaginations and raise their awareness of the universe. It is only once learners become aware of what is happening around them that their senses can transport them to new places and explanations about science based on how they feel and experience their environment. In so doing, they become connected to the universe in much the same way as the great scientific thinkers once experienced the forces of nature through their senses and made new contributions to the world of science.

SENSE EXPERIENCE ACTIVITIES

The following approaches are recommended as guidelines for assisting physical science teachers in enhancing and encouraging the use of the senses in the classroom:

THE OBSERVATIONAL APPROACH

Grambo (1994) points out that observation in science involves more than just a recalling of details of what precisely took place but also requires the observer to follow through by asking why a process unfolds in a particular way. He points out that this recall of detail needs to be followed by the question "Why?", which is crucial in solving scientific problems. In doing so, the teacher and learners as observers learn to filter out information that has no bearing on understanding an observed phenomenon. This is because the question "Why?" connects the observed event with a process of constant reflection on the reasons why things happen the way they do. This assists the learners in achieving a richer understanding of what they have observed. In other words, observation is more than just 'seeing' or 'looking' at something with the eyes. It must be performed in conjunction with brain function and all the senses—that is, touching and smelling, and sometimes even tasting and hearing.

Norris (1987) draws a distinction between observations for *'theory confirmation'* as opposed to observation for *'theory building'*. He states that observation has a dual role in science, that is, to build knowledge in the field of science (774) while also serving as the basis for testing specific knowledge claims and for arbitrating between conflicting claims. Theory-confirming observations in his view belong to astrophysical and starlight deflection observations, whereas theory-building observations belong to the observations found in textbooks that are open to scrutiny and scientific testability. For example, Thomson's observation of the electron was theory-building for Einstein's theory of relativity. Wilson maintains that scientists pay more attention to observations than to facts. This is because it is observation that determines which facts are important to focus on.

Wilson further emphasises the importance of the senses in the theory-building process in science. He argues that the superior quality of observations is made with the human senses compared to those made with instrumentation. He writes, "The further scientists are away from primary data in terms of pre-processing, the greater the potential for egregious error in interpretation" (Wilson 1987, 775). It is worth noting that not all scientific observations can be linked to the naked eye. For example, information-carrying mechanisms such as subatomic particles like electrons, protons, positrons, and so forth, require the other sense perceptions of touching, hearing and smelling. For example, when Dalton refuted Thomson's plum pudding model of the atom, he used a scintillation screen that produced visible observed sparks to detect the presence of the alpha particles that went straight through the gold metal. This discovery involves the use of all the sense organs. This brings me to the question: How can teachers improve the observational skills of learners?

Observational Strategies

Teachers can design activities which encourage learners to observe an event or object of their choice and then to give a report on the findings to the whole class. For example, some learners might have a deep interest in the ocean, whereas others might like a pet such as a dog or a cat or prefer a sport such as cricket, soccer or rugby. The activity must be formulated and structured in such a way that the learners first have to give a very general description of the observed phenomenon. For example, a learner who describes the ocean at the macroscopic level can describe the people on the beach, the colour of the water, the size of the waves or any other significant aspect or event. It is during this phase that learners are guided to use the appropriate discourse type, grammar, syntax, lexis and style to record their observations. This general description should make way for a more detailed and specific examination of what was observed. Finally, the macro-observational descriptions should lead to a focus on and description of microscopically specific details pertaining to the nature of the ocean, such as the molecular composition of the water, the bubbles (methane gas) that are produced by micro-organisms (methanogens) in the water, the nature and presence of salt and the type of chemical bonds between water and sodium chloride molecules. These observations should motivate the learner to reflect on how these bonds affect the temperature of the water, the specific heat of the water, ocean currents, the intervals between waves and perhaps how the wind speed and strength influence the way surfers use the environmental conditions to ride the huge waves. At this point the teacher can also introduce the learner to the Newtonian concept of tidal forces and how they affect ocean currents. Here the role of the teacher is to guide the learners to unpack the finer details in their reports. Gardner (2006) argues that such activities create a nurturing environment for the learner to cultivate a better understanding of the observed event.

This suggested activity can be extended by asking the learner probing questions about the nature and accuracy of, as well as the reasons for, the observations made. The purpose of such unsettling questions is to instil a measure of uncertainty and insecurity in the learners regarding the presumed accuracy of their observations. This, in turn, could motivate the learner to seek assistance or conduct independent research to gain a richer understanding of the observed phenomenon. When the learner has a clear understanding of what was observed, the event becomes fixed in his or her memory and could foster a level of awareness similar to that which informed the reasoned observations of scientists such as Newton, Dalton and Einstein and that led to their extraordinary discoveries and inventions. This activity could be followed by applying the skill of observation in more detail.

Sense-Experience Activity 1: Chemical Bonding
Chemical bonding forms part of every grade (10–12) in the FET band for physical science in the South African CAPS curriculum. The topic is often described by researchers as an important topic in the school science syllabus since almost every aspect of chemistry is built on the topic (Johnstone 1991; Taber 2011). Chemical bonding is the foundational issue in order to understand other more advanced related topics in science such as acids and bases, electrochemistry and in particular organic chemistry. All physical objects in the universe are made up of chemical bonds, which at a microscopic level determine the properties and behaviour of different objects. For example, the foods we eat, such as carbohydrates, proteins, lipids, and so forth, are made up of different types of complicated chemical

bonds that range from giant crystal lattices to infinitely small ions, peptide bonds and covalent bonds. Other examples and applications of chemical bonding include the different types of raw materials used to construct houses such as cement, metal or aluminium window frames and doors, the plumbing, roof trusses, and so forth, which lead to better and more durable products through the application of the principles of chemical bonding. The question is: How can teachers sequence a lesson on this topic that will require the learners to use their senses?

Creating a Context or an Experience for the Topic

Scenario
Hair chemistry is part of the daily realities of all the girls in this classroom. Tanya decided on washing her hair (representing the breaking of bonds) and asked Mpho to assist her in blow-drying her hair. Mpho remarked, 'I like the volume of your hair (bond formation—disulphide bonds). It looks so fresh and funky. I blow-dried it longer than usual so that it can maintain its volume for longer than usual (bond strength).' Disappointingly, much later into the night, as the temperature drops, Tanya realises that her hair lost some volume and started to shrink (collapsing of the disulphide bonds).

Rather than following the traditional top–down approach, where the teacher starts the lesson with an emphasis on the division between the four different bonding types (microscopic level) and the rules associated with constructing theoretical models of the specific bond types and leading finally to a discussion on the properties of different materials and objects, a bottom–up approach should be followed. For this purpose, as an introduction to the lesson, the teacher can create a context in which he or she draws on *an experience,* in the Deweyan sense, in which the teacher relates the scenario to the experiences as lived by the learners.

At this point, the teacher can start the dialogue with guiding questions such as: What types of bonds are formed when Mpho blow-dried Tanya's hair? To answer this question, the teacher can draw on the burning smell given off in the blow-drying process. This question will set the scene for more layered questions leading to deeper levels of understanding of the topic. For example, what is the nature and classification of disulphide bonds? Are they covalent or ionic bonds, and so on? The teacher can give the learners a task to formulate the differences between the types of bonds. This can be followed through with a discussion on the remark Mpho made about blowing Tanya's hair a little longer to gain an insight into bond strength and bond length, which is temperature dependent, as experienced when her hair shrinking. From that point onwards, the learners can be given a task in which they can compare the properties of covalent bonds as depicted in the scenario with ionic bonds as a starting point to unpack the science in the event relating to the different types of chemical bonding in nature. This approach will shift the focus of the lesson from the macroscopic event to the microscopic properties implicit in the scenario. From this point onwards, the teacher can guide the discussion to introduce phenomena such as bond strength and bond length and their uniqueness and relevance to the different bond types.

In another context, the learners can be introduced to different objects and materials that require careful inspection and dissection into smaller pieces. The teacher can request learners to categorise the different objects and materials into the respective bonding types. From this point onwards, the learners can be guided to do further investigations by describing the properties of the respective objects and materials in the different bonding types and comparing them with one another. At this point, the learners can investigate the influence of bond length on bond strengths and bond energy that keep the objects and material together and the magnitude of the forces required for separating the molecules. From this the learner can gain an insight into how bond strength and energy relate to the different types of bonds and which bond type is the strongest of the four.

Sense-Experience Activity 2: Acids and Bases

Creating a Context or 'An Experience' for the Lesson

Scenario
Let's pretend it is a Saturday afternoon and it is very hot. You (learners) are lying beside the swimming pool with a packet of hot potato chips sprinkled with salt and vinegar while your dad is busy adding pool acid to the swimming pool. Your mom is busy doing the laundry using her favourite washing powder while your dad is craving for a glass of orange juice. Later on that evening you take a bath using your favourite bath soap to remove the chlorine from your body.

From this event learners can be requested to do the following:

- Collect samples at home of the materials mentioned in the above scenario and bring them to the science classroom;
- Use their senses of smell, taste or sight (observation) and write down the physical properties of the substances;
- Group substances with similar properties together;
- Assign a name to each of the respective groups;
- Perform an acid base test with each item using litmus paper, universal indicator and a pH metre;
- Classify the different items using classical theories (e.g. Arrhenius theory) and compare it with the Lowry–Brønsted theory;
- Use chemical bonding to differentiate between strong and weak acids, and strong and weak bases.

These sense-experience activities outlined above make the theoretical and conceptual knowledge derived dependent on experience. The teacher activities following the scenario provide an ontological approach and interpretation of abstract conceptual elements to bring the learner to a fuller understanding of their personal experiences with objects in the real world. In this approach, dealing with the phenomena can assist the learner in understanding the beauty of science through forms, colours, smells and taste as they learn to understand nature through sensory inquiry.

CONCLUSION

This argument in this chapter is premised on the common belief that a human being has only five senses, although there might be more, but that either supposition supports the call for the use of the senses in the science classroom. As Locke (2009) points out, simple ideas could lead to major discoveries which the mind knows nothing about except for that which it becomes aware of through the senses. I have argued that the use of the senses and sensory perception has long been neglected by science teachers and it builds a case for harnessing the power of the senses by pointing out how this dominated the work and discoveries of some of the leading scientists in the world. Consequently, science teachers should rethink the way they deliver content to learners. Instead of handing down ready-made knowledge about the laws, principles and theories of science, they should consider enriching the teaching and learning of science by encouraging the full use of the senses in their classrooms. The reason is that sense-experience approaches (SEAs) have the potential to foster creativity, open-mindedness and critical thinking. The use of SEA might therefore lead learners to new insights and dispel firmly held false beliefs and perceptions.

In conclusion, the author acknowledges that the incorporation of SEA into the science curriculum will require major revisions in curriculum design and lead to significant changes in pedagogical practices. However, it is his deeply held belief that these revisions are long overdue and critically important to enrich the teaching of science by empowering and guiding learners to make full use of their sense organs in their pursuit of scientific knowledge.

Notes

1. A learner must get 30 % or more to pass physical science in South Africa.
2. Calcination is process where a metal is heated until it changes its state to a calx (the residual substance that remains after a substance has been combusted).

References

Baker, D. P., Goesling, B., & Letendre, G. K. (2002). Socioeconomic status, school quality, and national economic development: A cross national analysis of the "Heyneman-Loxley Effect" on mathematics and science achievement. *Comparative Education Revie, 46*(3), 291–312.

Bryson, B. (2003). *A short history of nearly everything.* London: Transworld.

Chabata, J. G. (2013). Sir Isaac Newton: The knight in shining armour. *Science Stars, 2,* 8–11.

Cohen, I. B. (1985). *Revolution in science.* Cambridge, MA: Harvard University Press.

Dahlin, B. (2001). The primacy of cognition—or of perception? A phenomenological critique of the theoretical bases of science education. *Science and Education, 10,* 453–475.

Donnelly, J. F. (2004). Humanizing science education. *Science Education, 88*(5), 762–784.

Dube, T., & Lubben, F. (2011). Swazi teachers' views on the use of cultural knowledge for integrating sustainable development into science teaching. *African Journal of Research in Mathematics Science and Technology Education, 15*(3), 68–83.

Feynman, R., Leighton, R. B., & Sands, M. (1965). *The Feyman lectures on Physics.* California: Addison-Westley.

Fleisch, B. (2007). *Primary education in crisis: Why South African schoolchildren underachieve in reading and mathematics.* Wetton: Juta & Co, Ltd..

Gardner, H. (2006). *Multiple intelligences: New horizons.* New York: Perseus Books.

Grambo, G. (1994). The art and science of observation. *Gifted Child Magazine, 2,* 9–11.

Goodson, I. (1994). *Modern educational thought: Studying curriculum.* Buckingham: Open University Press.

Hanushek, E. A., Jamison, D. T., Jamison, E. A., & Woessmann, L. (2008). Education and economic growth; It's not just going to school, but learning something while there that matter. *Education Next,* Spring, 62–70

Hattingh, A., Aldous, C., & Rogan, J. (2007). Some factors influencing the quality of practical work in science classrooms. *African Journal of Mathematics, Science and Technology Education, 11,* 75–90.

Heidegger, M. (1967). *Being and time* (J. Macquarrie & E. Robinson, Trans.). London: SCM Press.

Heidegger, M. (2002). *The essence of truth* (J. Sadler, Trans.). London: British Library of the Congress.

Husserl, E. (1970). *The crisis of the European sciences and transcendental phenomenology: An introduction to phenomenological philosophy* (D. Carr, Trans.). Evanston, IL: North-Western University Press.

Jardine, D. W. (1992). Reflections on education, hermeneutics, and ambiguity: Hermeneutics as a restoring of life to its original difficulty. In W. H. Pinar & M. Reynalds (Eds.), *Understanding curriculum as phenomenological and deconstructed text* (pp. 116–132). New York, NY: Teachers College Press.

Johnstone, A. (1991). Why science is difficult to learn? 'Things are seldom what they seem'. *Journal of Computer Assisted Learning, 7,* 75–83.

Kenzani, M., & Onwu, G. (2013). Comparative effectiveness of context-based and traditional approaches in teaching genetics: Student views and achievement *African Journal of Mathematics, Science and Technology Education, 17,* 50–62.

Knorr-Cetina, K. (1999). *Epistemic cultures: How the sciences make knowledge.* MA: Harvard University Press.

Koopman, O. (2013). *Teachers' experiences of implementing the Further Education and Training Science Curriculum.* Unpublished doctoral thesis. Stellenbosch University, Stellenbosch.

Le Grange, L. (2015). Rethinking learner-centred education: Challenges faced by the African Child when learning school science and mathematics. *Unpublished paper. Stellenbosch, Stellenbosch University*

Locke, J. (2009). *Of the abuse of words.* London: Penguin Books.

Martin, M. O., Mullis, I. V., Gonzalez, E., & Chrostowski, S. J. (2004). *TIMMS 2003 International Science Report.* Chestnut Hill, MA: Boston College.

McEwan, H. (2010). Narrative reflection in the philosophy of teaching: Genealogies and portraits. *Journal of the Philosophy of Education, 45*(91), 125–142.

Mji, A., & Makgato, M. (2006). Factors associated with high learners' poor performance: A on mathematics and physical science. *South African Journal of Education, 26,* 253–266.

Muller, R. (2015). *Truth about South Africa's mathematics and science education quality.* http:mybraodband.co.za/news/government/103677. 14 May 2015.

Muwanga-Zakes, J. (2008). *Is science education in a crisis: Some of the problems in South Africa.* Africa online magazine, www.scienceinafrica.co.za/scicrisis.htm.

Norris, S. (1987). The roles of observation in science: A response to Wilson. *Journal of Research in Science Teaching 24*(8), 773–780.

Onwu, G., & Stoffels, N. (2005). Instructional functions in large, under-resourced science classes: Perspectives of South African larger classes. *Perspectives in Education, 23*(3), 79–91.

Østergaard, E., Dahlin, B., & Hugo, A. (2008). Doing phenomenology in science education: A research review. *Studies in Science Education, 44*(2), 93–121.

Pickering, A. (1995). *The mangle of practice.* Chicago: The University of Chicago Press.

Reddy, V. (2006). The state of mathematics and science education: Schools are not equal. In S. Buhlungu (Ed.), *South Africa, 2005–2006* (pp. 392–416). Pretoria: HSRC Press.

Roth, M., & Bowen, G. M. (2001). Professionals read graphs: A semiotic analysis. *Journal of Research in Mathematics Education, 32,* 159–194.

Sadler, T. (2009). Situated learning in science education: Socio-scientific issues as context for practice. *Studies in Science Education, 45,* 1–42.

Schwab, J. (1959). *The impossible role of the teacher in progressive education.* Chicago: The University of Chicago Press.

Spaull, N. (2013). South Africa's education crisis: The quality of education in South Africa 1994–2011. Report Commissioned by CDE. Johannesburg: Centre for Development and Enterprise.

Taber, K. (2011). Models, molecules and misconceptions: A commentary on 'secondary school students' misconceptions of covalent bonding. *Turkish Science Education, 8*(1), 3–18.

UMALUSI Report. (2015). *Department of Basic Education.* Author: Pretoria.

Wilson, V. (1987). Theory-building and theory-confirming observations in science and science education. *Journal of Research in Science Teaching, 24,* 279–284.

Wong, D., & Pugh, K. (2001). Learning science: A deweyan perspective. *Journal of Research in Science Teaching, 38*(3), 317–336.

CHAPTER 8

Can a Phenomenological Approach Enhance Learning in Science in South Africa?

INTRODUCTION

A perennial problem in science education over the past few decades has been the perception that science is out of reach for many learners and out of touch with their daily lives (Ogunniyi 1987; Price and McNeill 2013). Consequently, many learners regard the prospect of pursuing a career in science as being for someone else, somewhere else (Price and McNeill 2013). Research into their views about school science reveals that many of them regard the field as being "socially sterile, impersonal, frustrating, intellectually boring, and dismissive of life worlds and career goals" (Aikenhead 2006, 26). This is demonstrated by the steady decline in the enrolment figures for the subject. For example, in South Africa, the Umalusi Reports (2008, 2014) indicate that a total of 217,300 secondary-school learners wrote physical science in 2008 compared with 184,056 in 2011 and 171,549 in 2014. The total number of learners enrolled for the subject in 2008 was 37.8 %, 35.3 % in 2011 and 32.7 % in 2014.

That this disturbing trend is not unique to South Africa is borne out by the fact that Osborne et al. (2010) observed the same trends in England and Wales. At the core of such concerns is the realisation that a nation's standard of achievement and competitiveness depends on a highly educated and well-trained scientific community. The current low intake of science learners therefore poses a serious threat to the economic prosperity of many countries. To meet this challenge, Hurd (2002) argues, it is

© The Author(s) 2017
O. Koopman, *Science Education and Curriculum in South Africa*,
DOI 10.1007/978-3-319-40766-1_8

165

necessary to design a curriculum that values lived experience as opposed to the mechanistic and instrumental way science is taught in most schools globally. Researchers such as Ogunniyi (1987) and Price and McNeill (2013) echo the growing concern over the instrumental nature of science teaching, the effects of learners being viewed as mere spectators in the science classroom and learners' belief that science is out of touch with their daily lives. Meanwhile, attempts at reforming the nature of science teaching are constrained by the enervating demands of having to prepare learners for content-based examinations testing rote-learning and memorisation skills. Investigating the conflict between school science and the learners' personal and cultural identities, Ogunniyi (1988) and Jegede (1999) conclude that unless learners' lifeworlds can be incorporated into the teaching of school science, learners will always experience science as being dogmatic, distant, sterile and untrustworthy. The researchers stress that school science must give learners an opportunity to experience science authentically, free of the legends, misconceptions and idealisations about the nature of the scientific enterprise. Aikenhead (2006) argues that such a reconceptualising of science teaching is imperative because many science teachers remain trapped in the traditional, content-focussed science curriculum designed to prepare learners for the science pipeline. Corroborating this, Mallya et al. (2012) describe how students have to endure painful experiences in science where the focus is essentially on rote learning, memorisation, and the reading and reciting of irrelevant definitions of science concepts. They echo the lamentation of learners who constantly ask, "Why do we have to learn this? What does this have to do with anything?" Conversely, Barton (cited in Mallya et al. 2012) describes the enthusiasm of learners living in extreme poverty when they were given the opportunity to engage in meaningful science. Barton explains how these learners were challenged to identify and build a structure needed at the shelter in which they lived. The final outcome of the practical proposals, such as the design and construction of a picnic table, mirrored who they were and what they wanted science to be. In other words, the final outcome of their projects flowed from their inner landscapes and lived experiences. In another project, Mallya et al. (2012) found that learners who struggled to score good marks in science and often failed to do their homework sacrificed their leisure time and weekends to complete their projects, as the focus of the projects was on their lived experiences.

THE CURRENT STATUS OF SCIENCE TEACHING IN SOUTH AFRICA

Despite the demise of the apartheid curriculum and the introduction of at least four curriculum revisions during the past 20 years, little has changed in the way science is presented to learners (Koopman 2013). The lessons continue to be based on ready-made knowledge and inconsequential facts far removed from the learner's everyday experiences. For example, instead of teachers explaining how to calculate the unknown volume of a gas, learners should be shown how to use gas laws to save lives on the roads when they travel with family. They should be taught how to build their own barometer when they are stranded on an unknown island to determine how high or low relative to sea level they are positioned. In this way, learners can link gas laws to real-life applications and put the necessary precautionary measures in place when they inflate the tyres of their cars. It has been found on occasions that learners want to participate in science lessons but cannot because the science curriculum glosses over the real world and social complexities learners are faced with. This raises the question whether giving more prominence to lived experience and the use of the senses in the science classroom would improve the quality of learning. The author believes that the static current notion that the study of science as mediated by a single authority figure (the teacher as the subject specialist and authoritative top–down purveyor of subject content) can construct the world and reality for the learner is fallacious. This misconception should make way for the dynamic realisation that the teaching of science should therefore confront this challenge to make science more practical, enjoyable and relevant to the daily lives of their learners, whose needs should be at the heart of the teaching and learning process. Koopman (2013) and Østergaard et al. (2008) maintain that it is important to assist learners in discovering the complexity of their lifeworld through scientific investigations involving deductive reasoning and making full use of the senses. The next section briefly explains how, for about half a century, the science curriculum in South Africa militated against the use of lived experiences in the teaching and learning of science.

CURRICULUM AND THE LIVED WORLD OF THE LEARNER DURING THE APARTHEID ERA IN SOUTH AFRICA

During the apartheid era (1948–1994), education in South Africa had two main functions, namely *qualification* and *socialisation*. According to Biesta (2010), *qualification* denotes the manner in which education adds value to the attainment of knowledge, skills and disposition, whereas *socialisation* is centred mainly on the citizenry, that is, where learners are trained to become part of the mainstream socio-political, socio-economic and moral movements of the society. The National Assembly Training and Education Department 550 (n.d.) curricula provided the basic pedagogical framework for managing the aforementioned two functions. Thus, the content of science was seen as a commodity or a product to be delivered by the teacher for consumption by the learners. Learners were mainly evaluated on the basis of how well they performed in the examinations which tested the content or 'what' of the science curriculum, with little regard for the 'who' and 'why'. The curriculum failed to bring the lived experiences of learners into the science classroom by disregarding the role and value of intellectual intuition, the use of the senses, learner uniqueness, and the learner's knowledge of the lived world. In other words, it failed to encourage a critical approach towards learning that would actively involve learners in the process of constructing knowledge. Similarly, it failed to empower the learners to use their senses to observe, record and demonstrate an understanding of the subject matter and to draw on and apply their own knowledge to the learning experience. Instead, the learners would leave the classroom cognitively unchallenged with only a shallow understanding of the world around them (Naidoo and Lewin 1998). As Jansen and Taylor (2003) rightly point out, this curriculum only served to destroy the originality, intellectual development and creativity of the learner.

CURRICULUM AFTER THE DEMISE OF THE APARTHEID SYSTEM (POST-1994)

The official demise of the repressive apartheid system in 1994 gave birth to the Department of Education's (DoE 1997) C2005 and all the Department of Basic Education's (DoBE) other curricula that followed in its wake. These included, for example, the RNCS 2005 (DoBE 2002), the NCS (2006) and the CAPS (2010), all of which were regarded as the educational route out of the sterility of apartheid education. Central to all these curricula was the belief that the learner and his or her lived world should be placed at the centre of the teaching and learning processes (DoE n.d., 1997; DoBE 2003, 2006, 2010). Hence, more attention had to be given to the *subjective* dimension of education.

Subjectivity embraces uniqueness and lived experience and regards human beings in their totality as free agents independent of social, political and moral movements (Sartre 1956). As such, it brought with it a new vision for education in general and more so for science. Instead of disconnecting the learners' subjective experiences from the pedagogical practices of teachers, curriculum planners now had to conjure up new ideas and approaches to link the two. Significance had to be given to the world of the learner with the aim of creating critical and reflective thinkers driven by the practical nature of the subject (NCS 2008). Furthermore, learners had to use the content and processes in science to develop a critical mindset to realise that science was personally and socially meaningful to them.

The Issue of Subjectivity

Research conducted by Østergaard et al. (2008), Dahlin et al. (2009) and Price and McNeill (2013) strongly suggests that the effective implementation of subjectivity has the potential to produce critical thinkers and invigorated, open-minded individuals. By contrast, the 'disruptive pedagogy' (Biesta 2010) of education as little more than a means to an end inevitably results in a failure to implement subjectivity effectively and therefore disrupts the natural 'becoming' of the learner. In Biesta's (2010) view, pedagogical approaches should neither interrupt nor disrupt learners' natural becoming or being but should protect them from such interruptions. Biesta (2010) shares Husserl's (1975) view that we all experience a sense of separateness or alienation from this world because we all have unique experiences. It is from these unique and rich daily experiences that learners formulate their own understanding of the laws, theories and principles of science, which they arrive at through the application of their senses. Teachers can weave some of these experiences into the planning of the daily science lessons to make the work real, interesting, appropriate and meaningful to the inquiring minds of learners. The following section explains the psychological theories of learning that have underpinned the learning styles since the advent and demise of the apartheid era in South Africa. The brief account is followed by a discussion of phenomenology as a learning theory.

Learning Theories

Each of the curricula discussed in the previous sections was rooted in a distinctive psychological theory. The apartheid curriculum was based on a behaviourist theory of development, whereas C2005 and its successors are underpinned by a constructivist theory. Each of these theories will now be explained by means of an extended metaphor, which is a powerful tool to clarify meaning and to bridge the gap between theory and application. Constandi (2010, 86) states that "metaphors are not just the concern of the poet or the literary critic ... but represent one of the ways in which many kinds of discourse are structured and powerfully influence how we conceive things".

Behaviourism

The behaviourist theory of development views the mind as a machine. The machine (e.g. an optical scanner) registers (sensory) experiences in the individuals receptive mind much in the same way that a teacher consigns knowledge to the learner's memory using different educational media such as an epidiascope or overhead projector. Alternatively, this theory can be likened to the way a computer stores ('the process of data input') bits of information and later retrieves them ('process of data output or retrieval') when needed.

Underlying the behaviourist metaphor of the mind as a machine, the associationist or stimulus-response theory views both the specific and the general cognitive structures as reflections of structures that exist outside the learner's world. Cognitive development is the result of guided teaching and learning. The efficacy of such theories is measured and limited by specific desired outcomes. For example, during examinations or tests, a learner's performance is measured by how well he or she can recite or regurgitate information from textbooks and class notes.

The Machine Metaphor in Science Education

This behaviourist metaphor represents the science learner as being isolated from lived experiences. Jegede (1999) argues that if the lifeworld of the learner is ignored, his or her framework of interpretation, which exists in the brain, is limited as it has no sensory image of the information. This does not mean that the learner will perform badly in science but that the science the learner is taught will not be assimilated into long-term memory. Rollnick et al. (2004) refer to this as the 'chunking' of information. These 'chunks of information' are complex schemata because the learner experiences a duality of thought, which takes place when a learner can hold unto two inconsistent ideas—one intuitive and the other formal—and sometimes possess genuine alternative conceptions which are unrecognised and undervalued together in his or her mind. According to Jegede (1999), duality of thought is a way of coping in a hostile learning environment, because a learner's immediate environment plays a significant role in his or her learning and determines how concepts are learned and stored in his or her memory. Furthermore, the dominant view on effective science teaching in South Africa ignores the impact of socio-cultural factors on learning, and as a result, learners might explain natural phenomena in ways that appear as non-rational in the perception of Western science but at the same time the learner experiences no contradictions in his or her conceptual system. In post-apartheid South Africa, these concerns eventually led to constructivist theories of learning as a supposedly fresh approach to science teaching and learning in the new curriculum.

Constructivism

The theory of constructivism represents a radical departure from the behaviourist approach. The differences between these two theories are marked. The first difference concerns the role of the *structure* of the subject matter in learning. Constructivism emphasises that the learning and teaching of *structure* (e.g. that of a scientific research report) is more productive than the mechanical mastery of facts and techniques. The second difference denotes the manner in which the learning of new ideas takes place so that the learner not only knows the facts but also knows how to apply them (the articulation, transfer and transformation of information) effectively in progressively more complicated forms. The third difference, the focus on intuition, involves critical and analytical thinking which leads to notions and discovery through inquiry. These differences greatly influenced the way science teachers had to (re)structure their lessons in the new curriculum.

Constructivist theory views the child not as a 'machine' but as a 'plant'. The reason for this metaphoric shift from machine to plant is that, just like a plant, the learner is in a constant phase of growth. Furthermore, a plant does not have a *permanent* wooden stem, leaves or flowers and is dependent on the synthesis of organic material for growth. A plant needs the loving care of a gardener to guide its shape and growth, and often the gardener has to remove all the dead matter to make space for new leaves and flowers.

As behaviourism began to fade in the 1960s in the USA, more prominence was given to Piagetian ideas. To Piaget (1960), thought is neither directly biological nor directly experiential but rather a reorganisation of the psychological structures that result from interactions between the organism and its environment. According to him, 'cognition' denotes structures that are internally organised wholes or systems of thought used as rules for the processing of information. As a result, learning takes place in cognitive isolation and it is not informed by day-to-day contingencies of experiences within the social and cultural settings. Therefore, within the Piagetian paradigm, the classroom is largely informed by the interaction between the conceptual domains of the home, community and school.

Novak's (1977) interpretation of Ausubel's work on meaningful learning challenges the idea of cognition advanced by Piaget. Novak is more interested in whether children develop cognitive structures or cognitive operations to make sense of their experiences. He believes that learners acquire a hierarchically organised framework of specific concepts that allows them to make sense of their experiences. Essentially, Novak argues that Ausubel's theory of meaningful learning, being dependent on a framework of specific concepts and their integration, provides a better explanation of the data from studies done than the Piagetian stages. Novak's work shifts the direction of research towards finding out how learners learn science.

Empirical data from research done over the last two decades confirm Novak's suspicion that learners learn and understand science differently than the scientific community. These findings question the basis of the learners' understanding of selected scientific concepts and the role of experience in their explanations. As a result of the latter, science teachers had to treat learners' conceptualisations of selected concepts in science in isolation in an attempt to reconstruct the learners' firmly held personal and cultural beliefs. Teachers' attempts to reconstruct these firmly held beliefs of learners failed dismally. The inability by teachers to change learner perceptions or notions of science paved the way for the different types of constructivism, namely social constructivism of the 1970s, radical constructivism of the early 1980s, socio-cultural constructivism of the early 1990s and critical constructivism of the late 1990s (for detailed explanation, see Duit and Treagust 1998). However, what is central to all these different types of constructivism is that each learner has his or her own view of reality. Furthermore, the learner's reality is influenced by social and cultural factors, as well as by physical and personal ones. Vygotsky's (1986) theory, which regards collective learning as primary and individual learning as secondary, is influential in this regard as it views this development as proceeding from the social to the personal spheres.

The Plant Metaphor in Science Education

In the science classroom in which the learner is metaphorically likened to a plant, the organic approach values the social and cultural environment within which the learner exists. Teachers who follow a constructivist pedagogy must be aware of the social and cultural knowledge learners bring into the science classroom so as not to complicate the learning process. This is important because in every society different worldviews interact. If school science is in conflict with the social and cultural worldview of the learner, it might result in cognitive perturbation (Jegede 1999). According to Gagné (cited in Coetzee and Imenda 2012), in a constructivist paradigm, the learning process is guided by a nine-step sequence of events: (1) gain the learner's attention, (2) inform the learner of the intended LO, (3) value and recall the learner's prior knowledge, (4) present the new content, (5) guide the learner in the learning process, (6) afford the learner the opportunity to follow the act, (7) provide feedback, (8) assess the effectiveness of the teaching and learning process and (9) enhance retention and transfer of knowledge. In such a learning environment, classroom activities focus on the *cognitive processes* of learners with the aim of restructuring firmly held beliefs (culture) and alternative conceptions regarding science. Most of the time, constructivists ignore the *spiritual* and *emotional* aspects of a learner's world. One of the main goals of theory-based constructivist pedagogy is to change the way a learner looks at the world and to reconstruct his or her perception and epistemic realities. The following three questions arise from this discussion:

1. How can a phenomenological approach enhance learning in the science classroom?
2. How does such an approach differ from a behaviourist and constructivist theory?
3. What does it offer that is different from these two theories?

Phenomenology as a Learning Theory

The Experiential Animal Metaphor in Phenomenology

As a science of lived experience, phenomenology can be associated with the metaphor of an animal in its natural environment. The animal is constantly growing and consciously alert to its environment through its sense of sight, smell, taste and hearing. Furthermore, 'instinct' (often described as a sixth sense) guides every movement of the animal with purpose and intent. According to Husserl (1975), cognitions begin with experience. In other words, we learn best from our experiences in the real world. When we are present in the world through experience, our senses connect our inner being to the space and place where we live. Hence, Locke (2009) avers that there can be no knowledge without experience. The individual's epistemological, emotional and psychological development depends on the data embedded in every experience. According to Merleau-Ponty (1962), a person projects meaning that is constitutive of his or her lived-world experiences. For example, watching closely how adults approach new technical problems reveals a process where they draw from experiences when they confronted and/or mastered a similar problem during their lives. Generally, they do not draw from their most sophisticated skills; instead, they draw from their experience that allows them to interact with the basic elements of the problems. They use these basic elements to build a foundation specific to the problem which guides their thinking on how to solve the complex aspects of the problem. Therefore, in the same way, phenomenology puts a stronger emphasis on the precognitive aspects of knowing which involve the senses and feelings that are dissimilar from the purely cognitive processes (Østergaard et al. 2008).

Phenomenology as Being and Acting in the World

Phenomenology is congruent with the theories discussed in the previous section, in that our daily actions are a direct result of a wider socio-cultural influence, but it attempts to balance the theoretical and conceptual explanations by connecting the theoretical knowledge to *being* and *acting* in the world as the basis for originality and creativity (Østergaard et al. 2008). As a theory of being (Heidegger 1967), phenomenology holds that the nature of existence is not cognitive but concrete in the sense that it involves real beings who are physically present in the world. This construction of reality has the potential to develop into a socially deterministic theory as people have different stances which are determined by their dominant cultural ideologies. For example, modern black learners in South Africa are more liberated than their counterparts on the rest of the African continent and free from their dominating cultural traditions. In the past, most African science learners would associate lightning with witchcraft or some kind of cultural phenomenon, and not as the discharge of electrons. The author's extensive interactions with black students strongly suggest that dominant cultural traditions are crumbling as increasing numbers of black students willingly accept and assimilate the scientific explanation of lightning in favour of traditional views. The reason is that people's knowledge of the world derives from their interaction with 'concrete physical things' in their immediate lifeworld (Heidegger 1967, 58).

PHENOMENOLOGY AND THE USE OF THE SENSES IN THE TEACHING AND LEARNING OF SCIENCE

As alluded to in Chap. 7, the senses play a major role in the meaning-making process and promote learning. Using their senses, individuals, for example, learn to classify objects as colourful, interesting or boring. Each object is classified according to specific criteria, which would be impossible without the use of the senses. For example, it is through the senses that the observer becomes aware of the external properties of plants and animals and various other objects. This identification of objects, which requires the effective application of the senses, is the 'data' which individuals use to frame their ideas. As individuals experience different objects, challenges and stimuli or make observations, they learn to compile their own rule book of how they think the world around them works. To do so, individuals use their senses to work through these events progressively to generate meaning and understanding. They use their lived experiences and senses carefully as 'scientific instruments' to dissect ontological clues linking the empirical with the aesthetic nature of things.

When the teaching of science is based on what children actually see, hear and feel when observing an event such as throwing a ball or a stone into the water, they instantly realise that a ball floats and a stone sinks. This experience penetrates deep into the surface mind and remains on the surface of the long-term memory because the external manifestation or empirical data of the phenomenon becomes their perceptual mindset. Although children observing such an event may not be familiar with the concept of buoyancy, the experience has the potential to transport them beyond the narrow bounds of what they have observed. They might start to question the differences in the molecular composition of the respective objects, which might prompt them to conduct further investigations. For this reason, Hunsberger (1991, 70) asks, "... Can an activity that can be so insight-giving, so much a stimulant to the imagination, lead to numbness and stupor?" The answer to this question is no; instead, like a drug it can have a variety of effects. Some of its most important effects are curiosity, creativity and independent learning. Thus, knowledge not only becomes part of the act of seeing but becomes a way of observing the experiential world around them. This leads to the question: How can the principles of phenomenology be incorporated into the science curriculum to revitalise the discipline and make it part of the lived experience of the learner? Figure 8.1 below gives a diagrammatical representation of the sequencing of events in a phenomenological paradigm.

Consciousness represents the learner's active thinking as derived from experience. According to Østergaard et al. (n.d.), the teacher should

1. allow the learner to use his or her experience to create a phenomenon for the content;
2. link the phenomena to the scientific explanation by using the learner's lifeworld;
3. use the scientific explanations and/or findings or descriptions to deepen the learner's understanding of the phenomenon;
4. expand on the science to deepen the learner's understanding of the phenomenon.

A Phenomenological Perspective on the Learner's Lifeworld

As Fig. 8.1 illustrates, all learning begins and ends with the lifeworld of the learner. This is because the perceptual information or mental residues in the memory carry information about the phenomena which are linked to a particular sensory modality. This information is funnelled into two possible streams: an *unresponsive stream* and a *responsive stream*. Both of these streams can be stimulated through insightful questioning to lead the

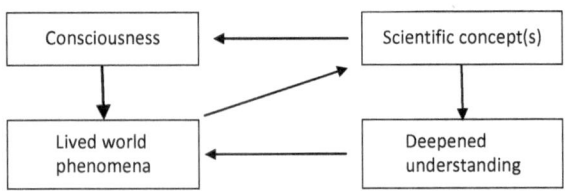

Fig. 8.1   Sequencing of events in a phenomenological classroom
Source: Adapted from Østergaard et al. (n.d.)

learner to a deeper understanding of the scientific phenomenon. Drawing on a learner's lived experience automatically activates the responsive stream, which leads to a deeper understanding of the phenomenon as the learner becomes more deeply aware of his or her surroundings. Science provides a rich insight into developing a closer interaction between the learner and his or her immediate environment. It is therefore important to work from an appropriate phenomenon that opens up the responsive stream to introduce the science because if the stimulus (experience) falls outside the receptor field, the 'neurons' short-circuit, leading to meaninglessness or pointless memorisation, so to speak.

Consequently, teachers should train learners at an early stage to investigate phenomena of interest by designing simple but thoughtful experiments to conjure up or refute hypotheses to expand their awareness in the real world. In so doing, teachers would release the learners' passion for asking questions and thus become co-inquirers with them. Teachers could also use the burning questions that learners bring into the classroom as a platform to develop lesson plans and classroom activities to stimulate debate about phenomena that are critical to them. These approaches have the potential to stimulate a deep interest in scientific knowledge per se and not merely *about* science in general as learners learn to reflect on their experiences. Therefore, instead of focussing on scientific correctness, learners should be allowed to free their imagination and raise their awareness about the universe. It is only once learners become aware of what is happening around them that their senses can transport them to new places and explanations about science based on how they feel and experience it. In so doing, they become connected to the universe much in the same way as the great scientific thinkers once experienced the forces of nature through their senses and made new contributions to the world of science.

Conclusion

The research reported on in this study calls for a phenomenological approach to the teaching and learning of school science. Phenomenology as a theory is not about knowing but about doing and being. Furthermore, it is way of connecting lived experience with science. The model presented (Fig. 8.1) offers an explanation for the processing of experience. It represents a view of the world through experience, and if the sensory modalities do not carry information about the event, the memory does not see it, rendering the learner incapable of making a cognitive leap. Conversely, if the responsive stream is activated, the experience becomes the object of consciousness which can be used as a hook to attach scientific knowledge. In so doing, the learner rises to a higher level of consciousness that creates a deeper state of awareness between the learner and his or her surroundings. It is worth noting that the study also acknowledges the theories of behaviourism and constructivism and their value to the teaching and learning process. However, it is important to note the constant changes in society and how the theoretical lenses with which we view the world also need to be adjusted.

Consequently, science teachers should rethink the way they deliver content to learners. Instead of handing down ready-made knowledge about the laws, principles and theories of science, they should give consideration to enriching the teaching and learning of science by encouraging the full use of the senses in their classrooms. The reason is that phenomenological approaches have the potential to foster creativity, open-mindedness and critical thinking. The use of lived experience, coupled with the senses, has the potential to lead learners to new insights and dispel deeply rooted false beliefs and perceptions.

In conclusion, drawing from his experiences as a learner, student, teacher and teacher educator of science, a phenomenological approach can enhance the learning of science in South Africa. He is convinced that these revisions are long overdue and critically important to enrich the teaching of science by empowering our learners.

REFERENCES

Aikenhead, G. S. (2006). *Science education for everyday life: Evidence-based practices.* New York: Teachers College Press.

Biesta, G. J. (2010). Education after the death of the subject: Levinas and the pedagogy of interruption. In Z. Leonardo (Ed.), *The handbook of cultural politics and education* (pp. 265—2289). Rotterdam: Sense Publishers.

Coetzee, S., & Imenda, S. (2012). Effects of outcomes-based education and traditional lecture approaches in overcoming alternative conceptions in physics. *African Journal of Research in Mathematics, Science and Technology Education, 16*(2), 145–157.

Constandi, S. (2010). Meandering through my epistemological patchwork quilt: A narrative inquiry of my landscapes of learning. *Journal of Philosophy and History of Education, 60,* 89–92.

Dahlin, B., Østergaard, E., & Hugo, A. (2009). An argument for reversing the bases of science education: A phenomenological alternative to cognitionism. *Nordina, 5*(2), 201–215.

Department of Basic Education. (2002). *Revised National Curriculum Statement: Grades R–9 (Schools): Natural Sciences.* Pretoria: Author.

Department of Basic Education. (2003). *Physical Sciences National Curriculum Statement. Grades 10–12 (General policy).* Pretoria: Author.

Department of Basic Education. (2006). *Physical Sciences National Curriculum Statement: Grades 10–12 (General).* Pretoria: Author.

Department of Basic Education. (2010). *Curriculum and Assessment Policy Statement: Physical Sciences (CAPS).* Pretoria: Author.

Department of Education. (1997). *Curriculum 2005.* Retrieved from http://www.polity.org.za/govdocs/misc/curr2005html

Department of Education. (n.d.). *National Assembly Training and Education Department (NATED) interim core syllabus for Physical Sciences (HG, SG & LG).* Pretoria: Author.

Duit, R., & Treagust, D. (1998). Learning in science—From behaviourism towards social constructivism and beyond. In B. Fraser. (Ed.), *International handbook of science education.* Dordrecht: Kluwer Academic.

Hansberger, M. (1991). Time and text. In W. H. Pinar & M. Reynalds (Eds.), *Understanding curriculum as phenomenological and deconstructed text* (pp. 64–91). New York, NY: Teachers College Press.

Heidegger, M. (1967). *Being and time* (J. Macquarrie & E. Robinson, Trans.). London: SCM Press.

Hurd, P. D. (2002). Modernizing science education. *Journal of Research in Science Teaching, 39*(1), 3–9.

Husserl, E. (1975). *The Paris lectures* (P. Koesterbaum, Trans.). The Hague: Martinus Nijhoff.

Jansen, J., & Taylor, N. (2003). Educational change in South Africa 1994–2003: Case studies in Large scale education reform. *Country Studies Education Reform and Management Publication Series, 2*(1), 1–96.

Jegede, O. (1999). Science education in nonwestern cultures: Towards a theory of collateral learning. In L. Semali & J. Kincheloe (Eds.), *What is indigenous knowledge? Voices from the academy* (pp. 119–142). New York: Falmer Press.

Koopman, O. (2013). Teachers' experiences of implementing the Further Education and Training science curriculum. Unpublished Doctoral Thesis, Stellenbosch University, Stellenbosch.

Locke, J. (2009). *Of the abuse of words.* London: Penguin Books.

Mallya, A., Menssah, F. M., Contento, I. R., Koch, P. A., & Barton, A. C. (2012). Extending science beyond the classroom door: Learning from students' experiences with the choice, control and change (C3) curriculum. *Journal of Research in Science Teaching, 49*(2), 244–269.

Merleau-Ponty, M. (1962). *Phenomenology of perception* (C. Smith, Trans.). London: Routledge and Kegan Paul.

Naidoo, P., & Lewin, K. M. (1998). Policy and planning of Physical Science education in South Africa: Myths and realities. *Journal of Research in Science Teaching, 35*(7), 729–744.

Novak, J. D. (1977). *A theory of education*. Ithaca, NY: Cornell University Press.

Ogunniyi, M. (1987). Conceptions of traditional cosmological ideas among literate and non literate Nigerians. *Journal of Research in Science Teaching, 24*(2), 107–117.

Ogunniyi, M. (1988). Adapting western science to traditional African culture. *International Journal of Science Education, 10*(1), 1–9.

Osborne, J., Simon, S., & Collins, S. (2010). Attitudes towards science; A review of the literature and its implications. *International Journal of Science Education, 25*(9), 1049–1079.

Østergaard, E., Dahlin, B., & Hugo, A. (2008). Doing phenomenology in science education: A research review. *Studies in Science Education, 44*(2), 93–121.

Østergaard, E., Dahlin, B., & Hugo, A. (n.d.). From phenomenon to concept: Designing phenomenological science education. *6th IOSTE Symposium for central and Eastern Europe.*

Piaget, J. (1960). The general problem of the psychological development of the child. In J. M. Tanner & B. Inhelder (Eds.), *Discussion on child development* (Vol. 4). New York: International Universities Press.

Price, J. F., & McNeill, K. L. (2013). Towards a lived science curriculum in intersecting configured world: An exploration of individual meaning in science education. *Journal of Research in Science Teaching, 50*(5), 501–529.

Rollnick, M., Allie, A., Buffler, A., Campbell, B., & Lubben, F. (2004). Development and application of a model for students' decision making in laboratory work. *African Journal of Research in Mathematics, Science and Technology Education, 8*(1), 13–27.

Sartre, J. (1956). *Being and nothingness.* (H. Barnes, Trans.). New York, NY: Washington Square Press.

Umalusi Report. (2008). Department of Basic Education. Pretoria: Author.

Umalusi Report. (2014). Department of Basic Education. Pretoria: Author.

Vygotsky, L. (1986). Though and language. In A. Kozulin (Ed.). Cambridge, MA: MIT Press.

Index[1]

[1] Note: Page numbers with "n" denote notes.

© The Author(s) 2017   181
O. Koopman, *Science Education and Curriculum in South Africa*,
DOI 10.1007/978-3-319-40766-1